DRAG AND DROP
MS Excel 2010

Davinder Singh Minhas

STERLING PUBLISHERS PVT. LTD.
A-59, Okhla Industrial Area, Phase-II, New Delhi
Ph.: 26386165, 26387070, 26386209
Fax: 91-11-26383788
E-mail: mail@sterlingpublishers.com
Website: www.sterlingpublishers.com

ISBN: 978-81-207-5738-7
© 2011, MS-Excel 2010

All rights reserved. No part of this publication may be reproduced, stored in a retrieval system, or transmitted, in any form or by any means, electronic, mechanical, photocopying, recording or otherwise, without the prior permission of the original publishers.

Printed at Sterling Publishers Private Limited., New Delhi-110020. India

Contents

Introduction	5
Creating worksheets	10
Formatting workbook	21
Formula and function	26
Charts in Excel	36
Printing worksheet	38

1 Introduction

MICROSOFT EXCEL 2010

Microsoft Excel is a powerful **spreadsheet program** that allows you to organize data, complete calculations, make decisions, graph data and develop reports.

Excel allows you to organize data in **rows** and **columns**. These rows and columns are collectively called a **worksheet**. For years, people used manual methods, such as those performed with pencil and paper, to organize data in rows and columns. The data in an electronic worksheet is organized in the same manner as it is done in a manual worksheet.

Just like MS-Word software, spreadsheet software has basic features to help you create, edit and format worksheets.

A spreadsheet file is like a notebook that has 255 individual worksheets. On each worksheet, data is organized vertically in columns and horizontally in rows. Each worksheet typically has 16384 columns and 1048576 rows.

A **letter** identifies each column, and a **number** identifies each row.

The column letters begin with **A** and end with **XFD**; row numbers begin with **1** and end with **1048577**. Only a small fraction of these columns and rows can be displayed on the screen at one time. To view a different part of a worksheet, you can scroll to display it on your screen.

The intersection of a column and a row is called a **cell**. A cell is the basic unit of a worksheet into which you enter data. Cells are identified by the column and row in which they are located. For example, the intersection of **column C** and **row 5** is referred to as **cell C5**. Cells may contain three types of data: labels (text), values (numbers) and formulas.

FEATURES OF MS-EXCEL

Edit and format data

Excel allows you to efficiently enter, edit and format data in a worksheet. You can quickly enter a series of numbers, find and replace data or check data for spelling errors. You can also make data stand out in a worksheet by adding borders or changing the font, color, style or alignment of the data.

Use formula and functions

Formulas and functions allow you to perform calculations and analyse data in a worksheet. Common calculations include finding the sum, average or total number of values in a list. As you work, Excel checks your formulas for problems and can help you correct common errors in them.

Print worksheets

You can produce a paper copy of a worksheet you create. Before printing, you can check on your screen how the worksheet will look when printed. Excel also allows you to adjust the margins or change the size of printed data.

Create charts and objects

Excel helps you create colourful charts from worksheet data to visually display the data. You can also create objects, such as AutoShapes, WordArt and diagrams, to enhance the appearance of a worksheet and illustrate important concepts.

STARTING MS-EXCEL

To start Excel in Windows Vista, follow these steps:

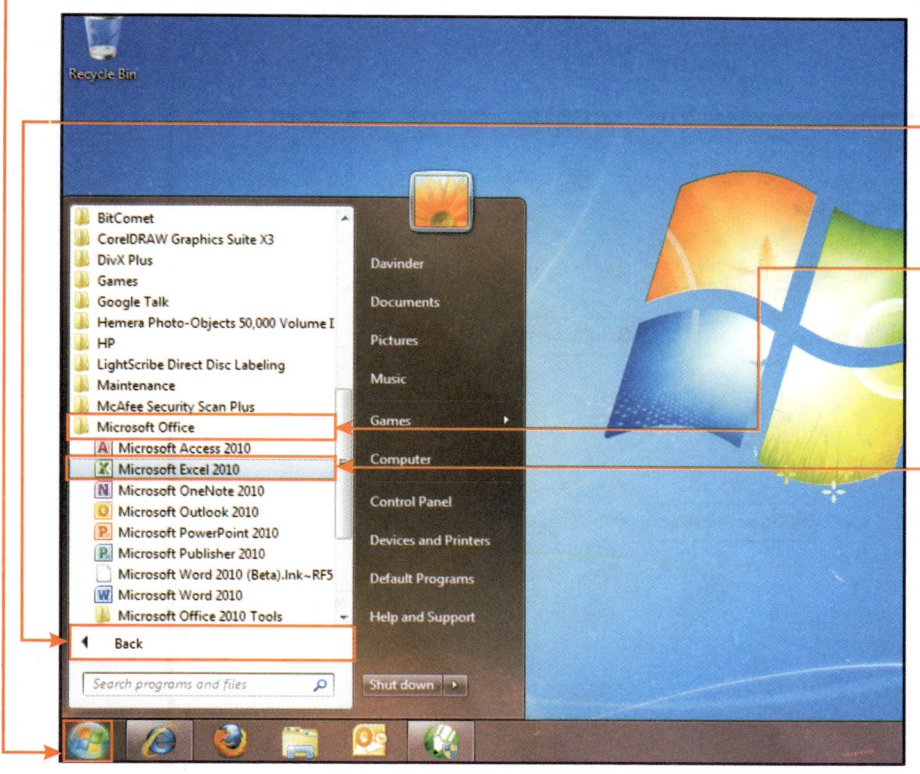

1. Click on the **Start** button. The Start menu will appear.

2. Click on **All Programs**.

3. Click on **Microsoft Office**.

4. Click on **Microsoft Office Excel 2007**.

The Excel Workbook will appear.

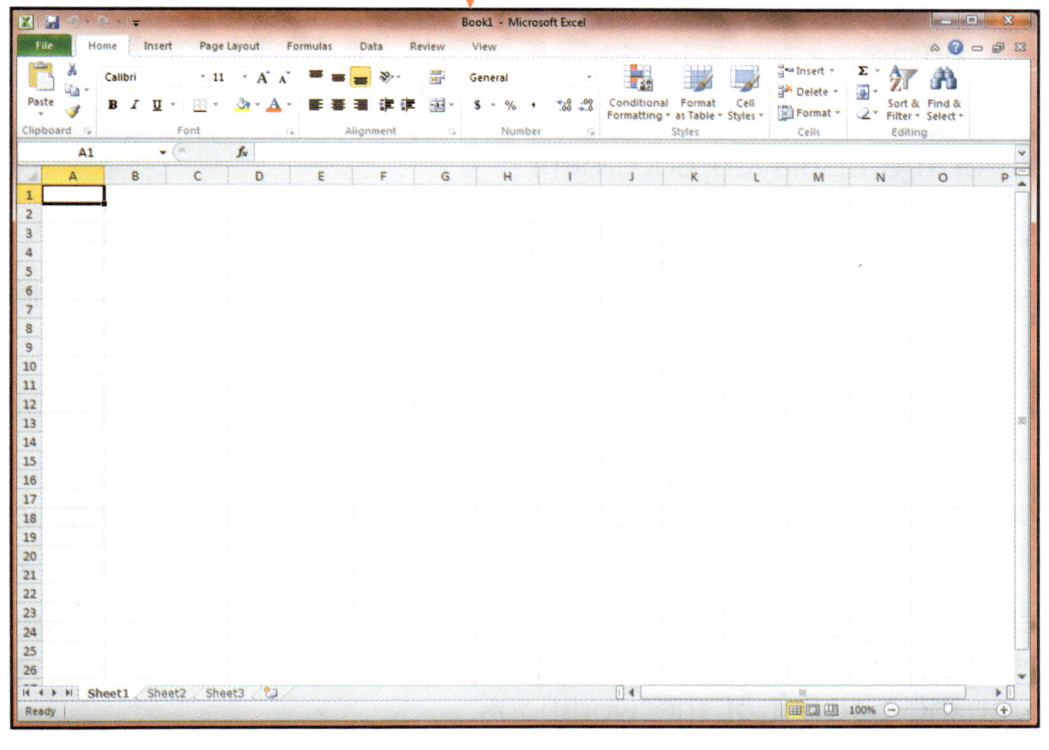

*An empty workbook titled **Book 1** is displayed in the Excel window.*

Drag and Drop Series

THE EXCEL WINDOW

The Excel window displays many items that you can use to create and work with your workbook.

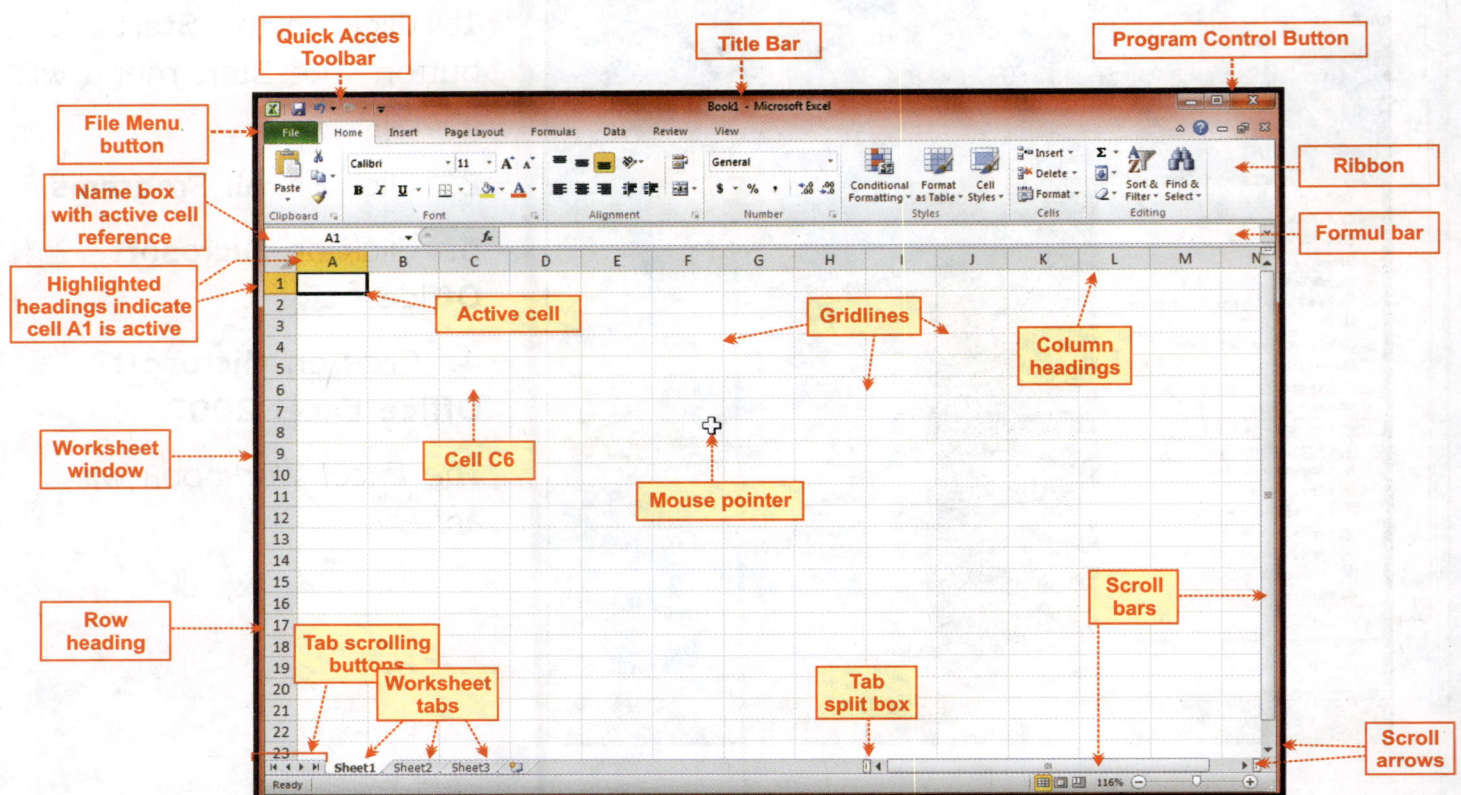

When you open the Excel program, a blank workbook is displayed and it is called a **Book**. The **workbook** looks like a notebook.

Title bar shows the name of the displayed document.

File Menu Button displays the menu of file commands, such as New and Open.

Quick Access Toolbar displays quick access buttons to the Save, Undo, and Redo commands.

Ribbon displays groups of related commands in tabs. Each tab offers shortcut buttons to common tasks.

Program Window Controls buttons are used to minimize the program window, restore the window to full size, or close the window.

The workbook contains sheets called worksheets. A new workbook contains three worksheets. You can also add additional worksheets. Each sheet has a name displayed on a **sheet tab** at the bottom of the workbook.

8

A worksheet is organized into a **rectangular grid** containing columns (vertical) and rows (horizontal). A column letter above the grid, also called **column heading**, identifies each column. A row number on the left side of the grid, also called **row heading**, identifies each row.

The intersection of each column and row in a worksheet is called a cell.

A cell is referred to by its unique address or **cell reference**, which are the coordinates of the intersecting column and row. To identify a cell, specify the column letter first, followed by the row number. For example, cell reference **C6** refers to the cell located at the intersection of column **C** and row **6**.

A cell in your worksheet is activated or selected for entering data into it. The **active cell** in the picture is **A1**. The active cell is identified in three ways.

- First, a heavy border surrounds the cell;
- Second, the active cell reference is displayed immediately above column A in the Name box and
- Third, the column heading A and row heading 1 is highlighted, so that it is easy to distinguish an active cell.

The horizontal and vertical lines representing rows and columns on the worksheet are called **gridlines**. Gridlines allow us to see and identify each cell within a worksheet.

The **mouse pointer** in the earlier picture has the shape of a block plus sign. The mouse pointer is displayed as a **block plus sign**, whenever it is located in a cell on the worksheet. The mouse pointer turns into a **block arrow**, whenever you move it outside the worksheet or when you drag cell contents between rows or columns.

A worksheet window allows you to view the portion of the worksheet displayed on the screen. Below and to the right of the worksheet window are the **scroll bars**, **scroll arrows** and **scroll boxes**, which you can use to move the window around to view different parts of the active worksheet.

2 Creating worksheet

CHANGING THE ACTIVE CELL

You can make any cell in your worksheet the active cell. An active cell has a heavy border around it. You enter data into the active cell.

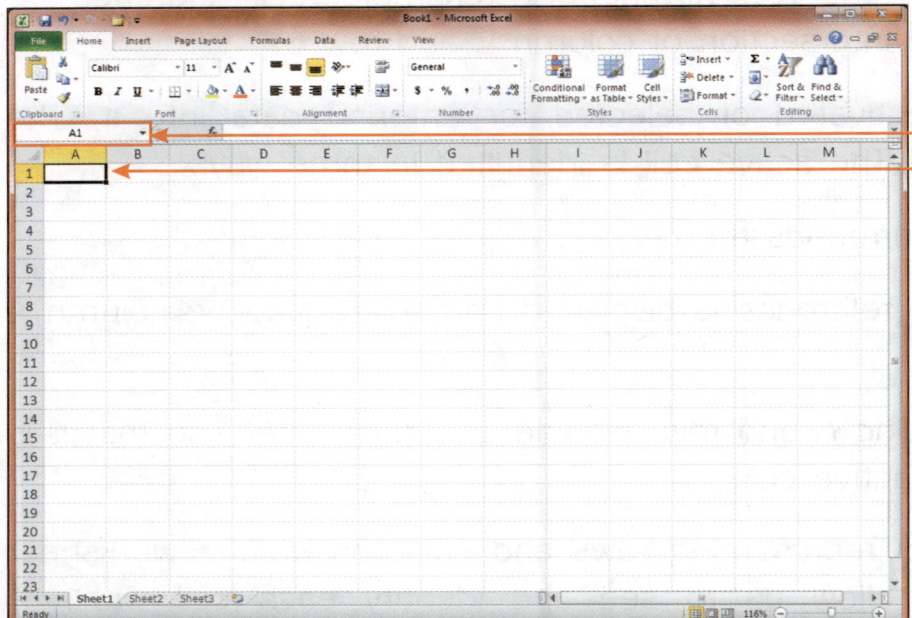

- The active cell displays a thick border.

- The cell reference for the active cell appears in this area. A cell reference identifies the location of each cell in a worksheet and consists of a column letter followed by a row number. (example: A1).

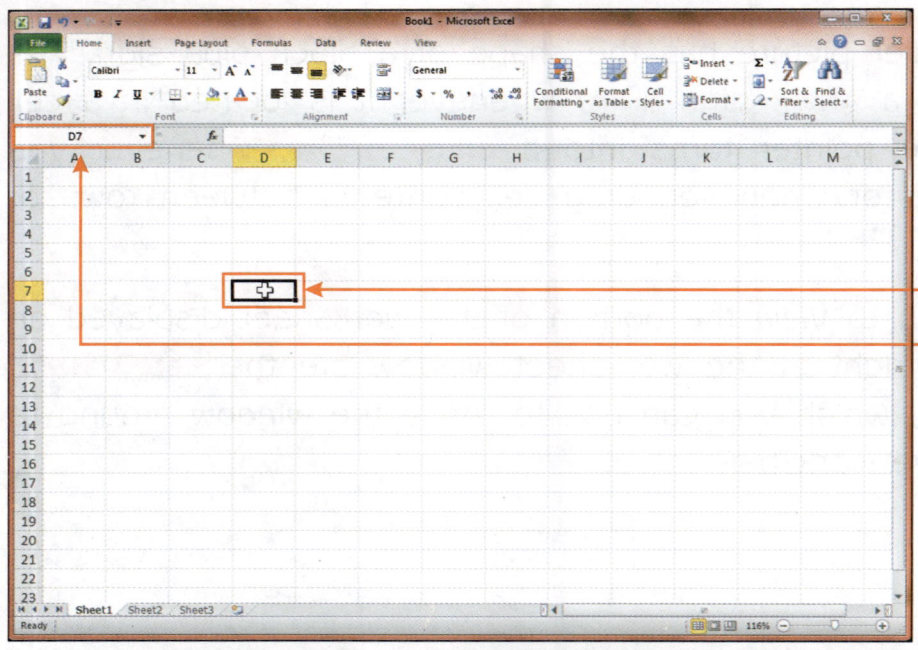

1. Click on the cell you want to make active.

   *You can also press **arrow keys** on the keyboard to change the active cell.*

- The **cell reference (D7)** for the new active cell appears in this area.

10

ENTERING DATA

You can enter data into your worksheet quickly and easily.

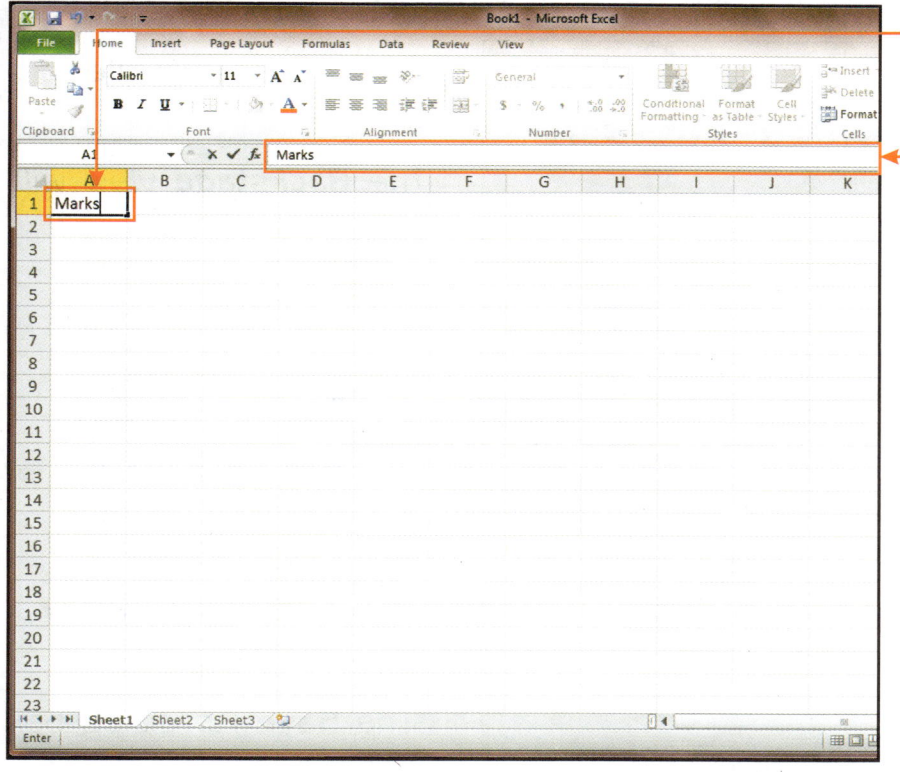

1. Click on the cell where you want to enter data. Then type the data.

The data you type appears in the active cell and in the formula bar.

If you make a typing mistake while entering data, press the Backspace key in the keyboard to remove the incorrect data. Then type the correct data.

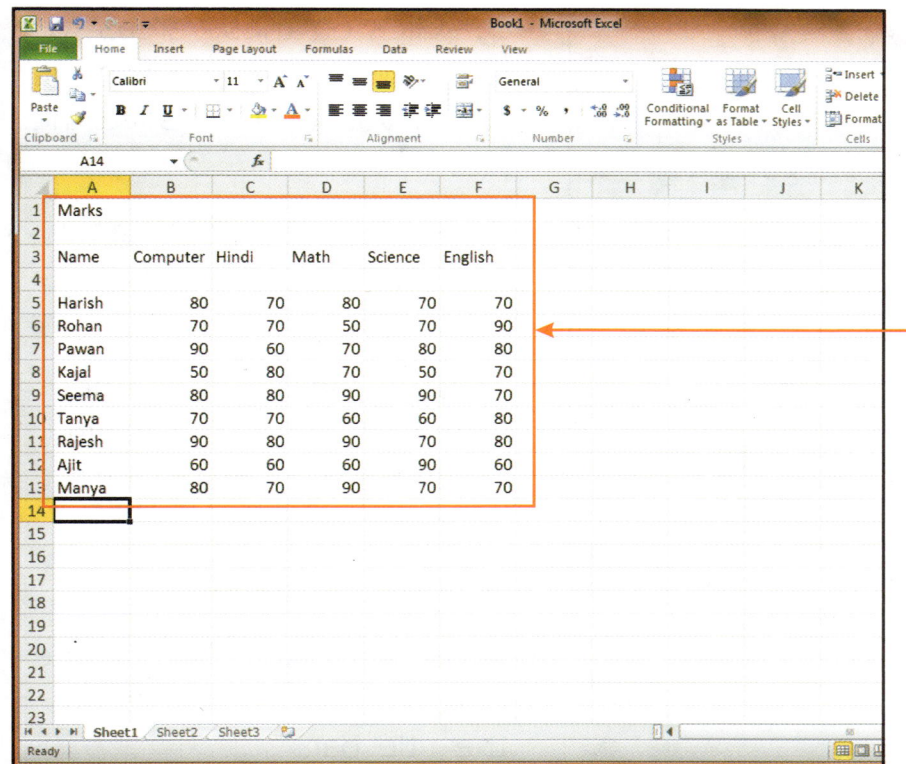

2. Press the **Enter** key to enter the data and move down one cell.

*To enter the data and move one cell in any direction, press **arrow** keys in the keyboard.*

3. Repeat steps 1 and 2 until you finish entering all your data.

Drag and Drop Series

SAVING A WORKBOOK

You can save your workbook for future use. Saving a workbook allows you to review and edit the data later. Saved file can be used on other computers also.

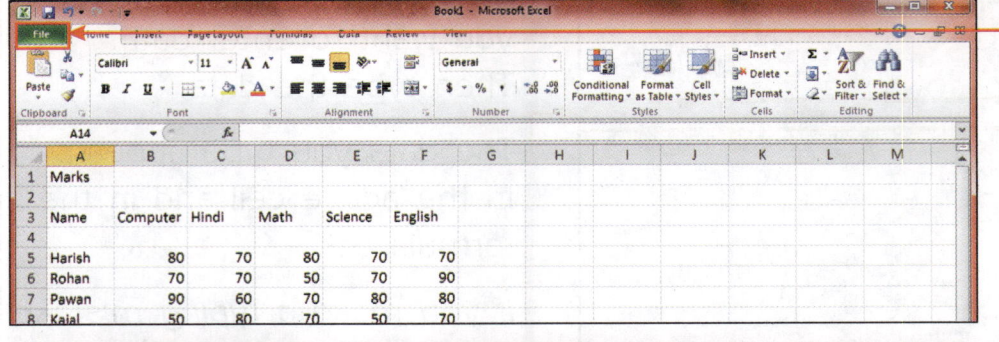

1. Click on the **File** tab.

   *The **Backstage** view will appear.*

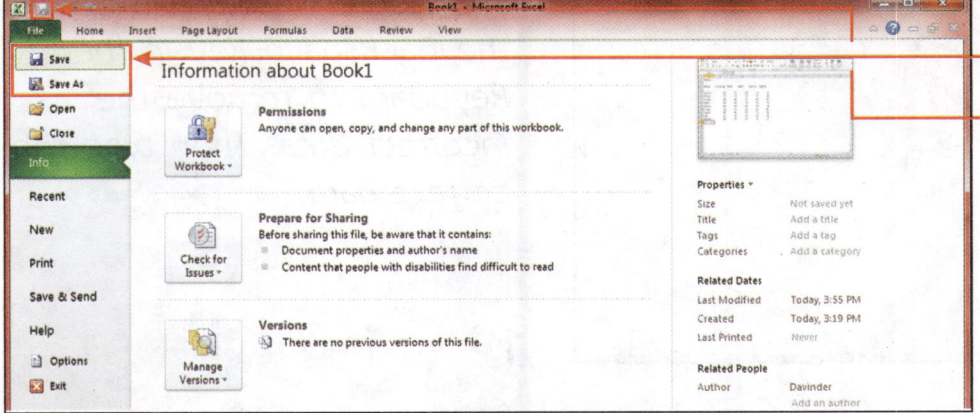

2. Click on the **Save** or **Save As** button.

   You can click on the **Save** button [🖫] on **Quick Access toolbar** to save the file.

   The **Save As** dialog box appears.

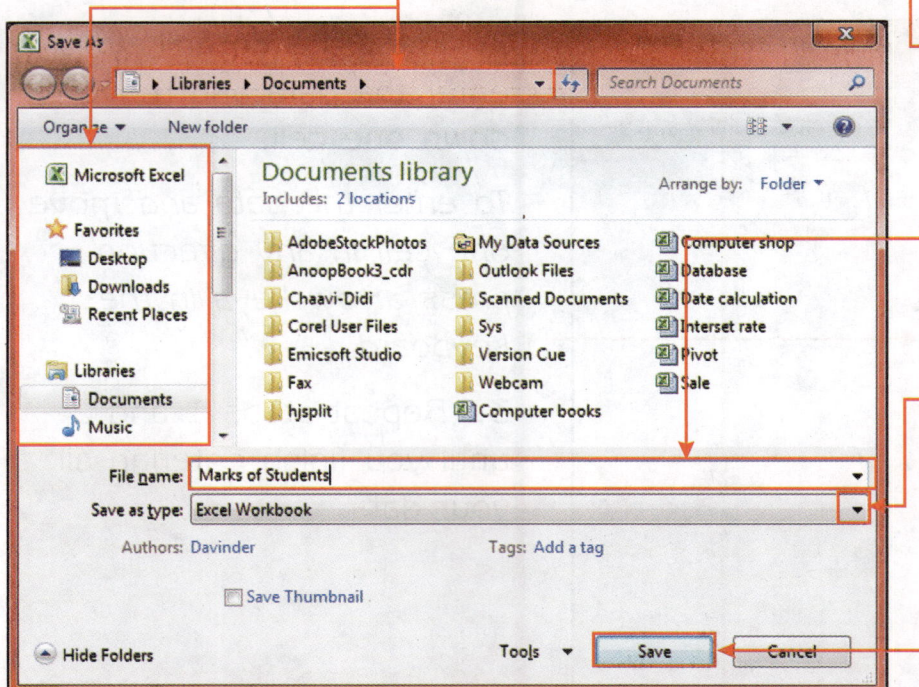

3. Click on these areas to navigate to the folder in which you want to save the file.

4. Click on the **File name** text box and type a name for the file.

   To save the file in another format, click on the down arrow **Save as type** and choose a format.

5. Click on **Save**.

   Excel saves the file and the new file name appears on the title bar.

12

CLOSING A WORKBOOK

You can close the workbook to remove it from your screen. Closing a workbook does not mean that you are exiting the Excel program.

Before closing a workbook, you should save any changes you made to the workbook.

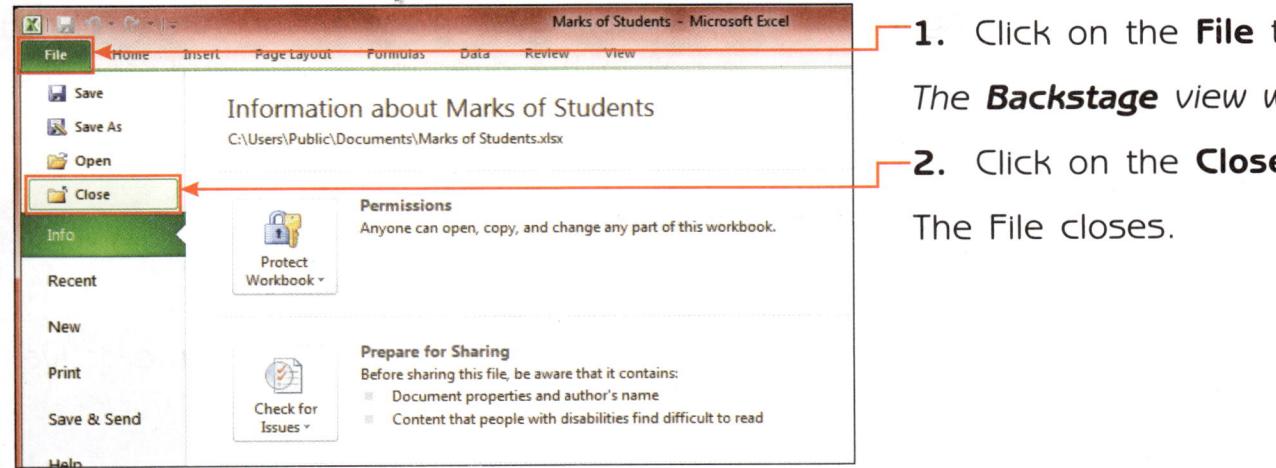

1. Click on the **File** tab.

   *The **Backstage** view will appear.*

2. Click on the **Close** button.

   The File closes.

OPENING A SAVED WORKBOOK

You can open a saved workbook to view the workbook on your screen. This allows you to make changes to the workbook.

1. Click on the **File** tab. The **Backstage** view will appear.
2. Click on the **Open** button.

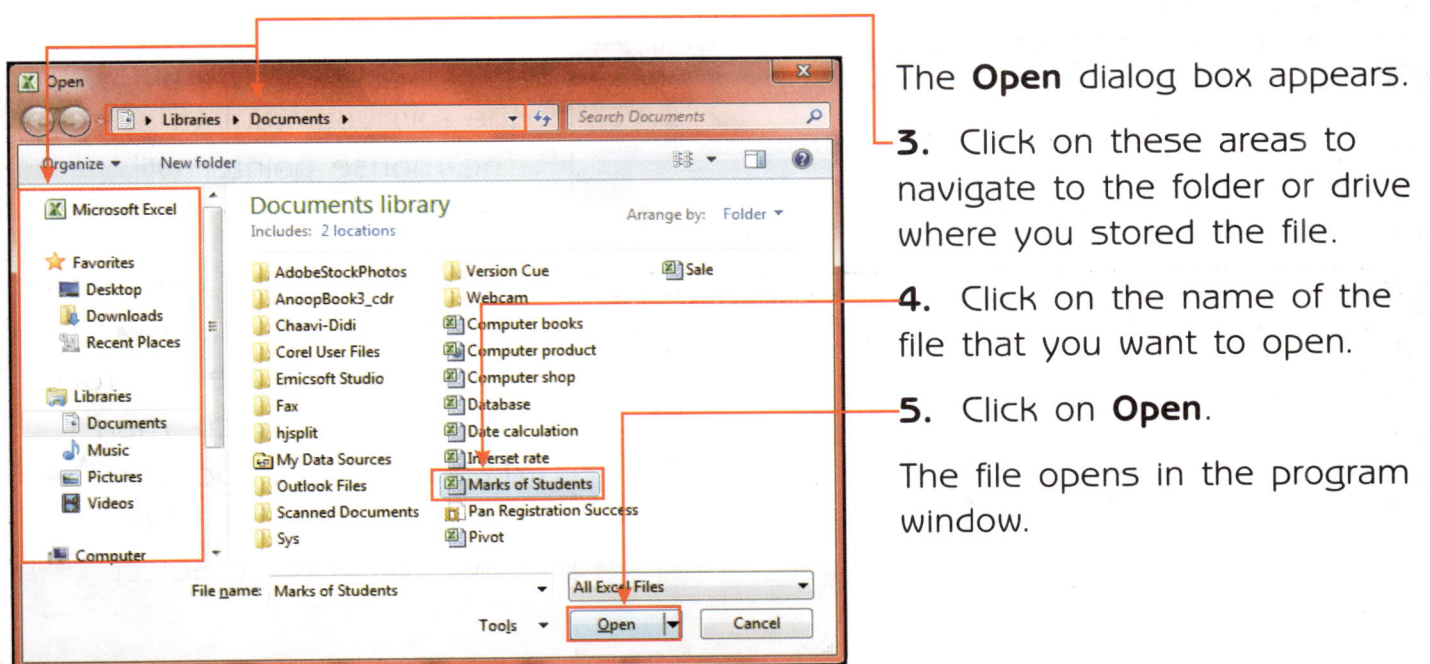

The **Open** dialog box appears.

3. Click on these areas to navigate to the folder or drive where you stored the file.

4. Click on the name of the file that you want to open.

5. Click on **Open**.

The file opens in the program window.

Drag and Drop Series

SELECTING CELLS

You must select a cell before entering data into it. The easiest way to select a cell (make it active) is to use the mouse to move the block plus sign to the cell and then click on it.

An alternative method of selecting a cell in a worksheet is by using the arrow keys that are located just to the right of the typewriter keys on the keyboard. An arrow key selects the cell adjacent to the active cell in the direction of the arrow on the key.

To select a cell

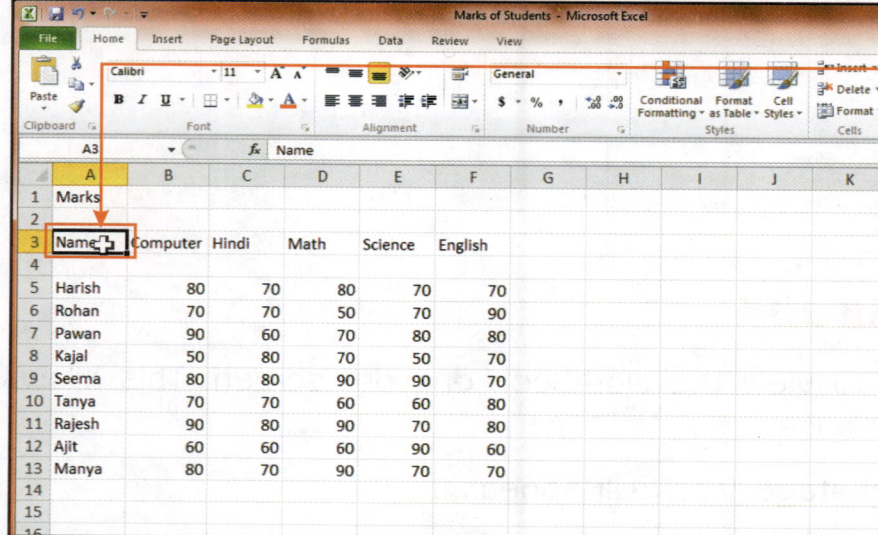

1. Click on the cell you want to select.

   The cell becomes the active cell and displays a thick border.

To select a row

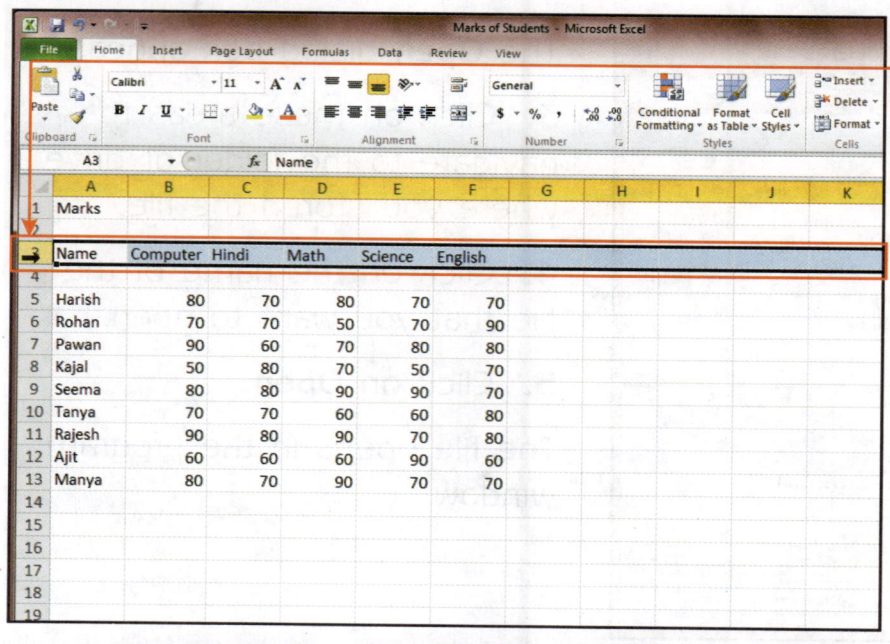

1. Click on the number of the row you want to select. The mouse pointer will change its shape (➔).

   To select multiple rows, place your mouse pointer (➔) on the number of the first row you want to select. Then drag the mouse pointer (➔) until you highlight all the rows you want to select.

To select a column

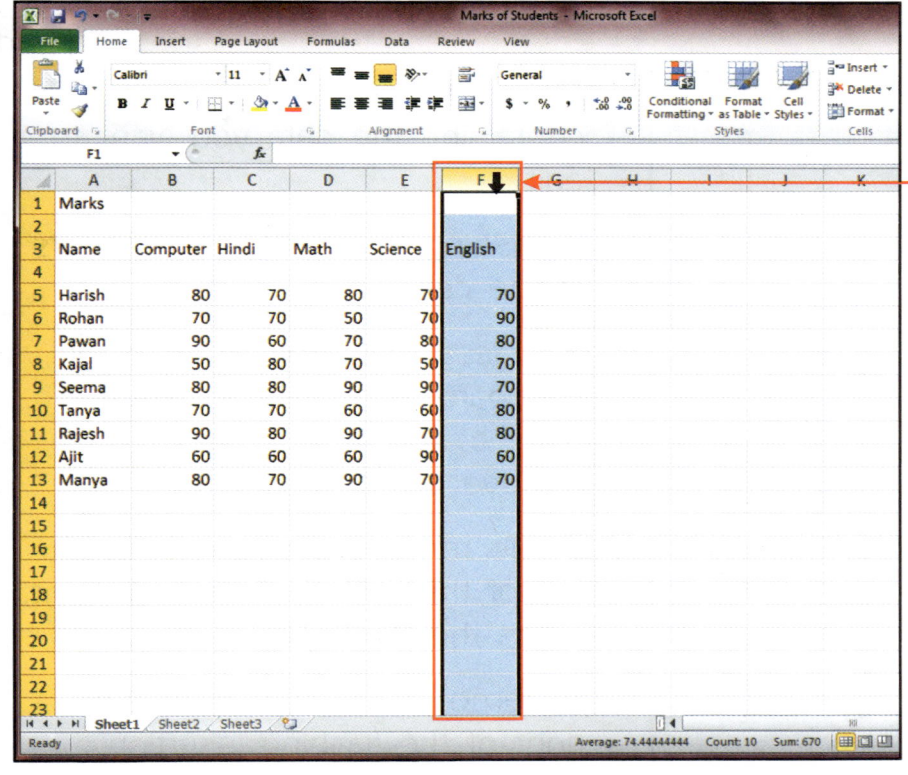

1. Click on the letter of the column you want to select. The mouse pointer will change its shape (↓).

To select multiple columns, position the mouse pointer (↓) on the letter of the first column you want to select. Then, drag the mouse pointer (↓) until you highlight all the columns you want to select.

To select a group of cells

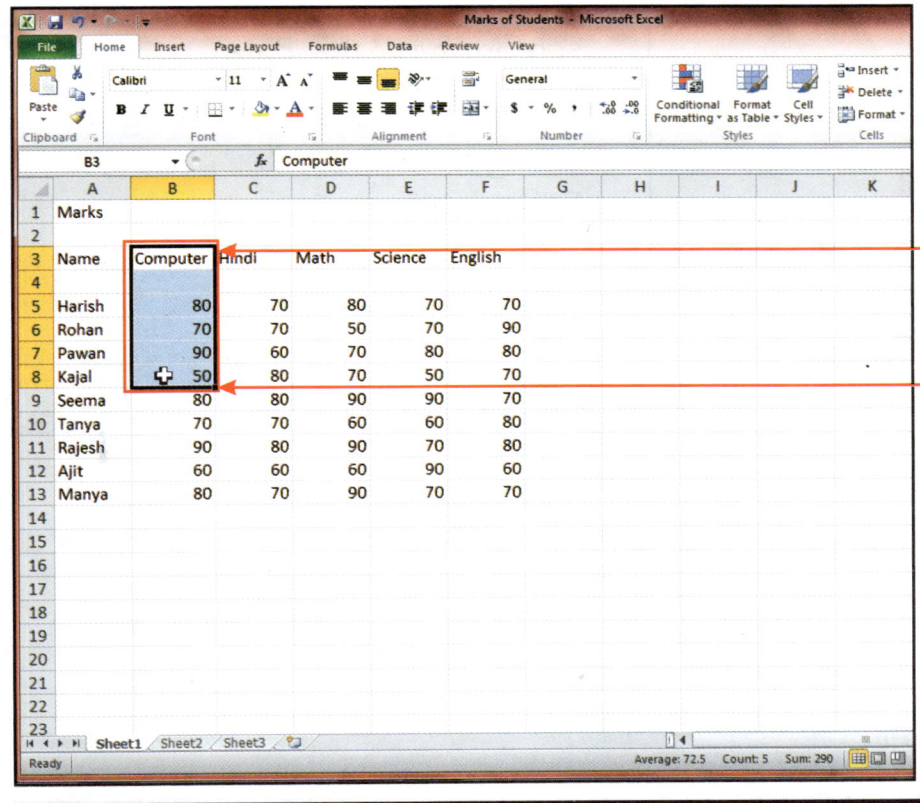

1. Place your mouse pointer (✢) on the first cell, you want to select.

2. Drag the mouse (✢) until you highlight all the cells, you want to select.

*To select multiple groups of cells, press and hold down the **Ctrl** key as you repeat steps **1** and **2** for each group of cells you want to select.*

Drag and Drop Series

EDITING DATA IN WORKBOOK

You can edit data in your worksheet for correcting a mistake or updating data.

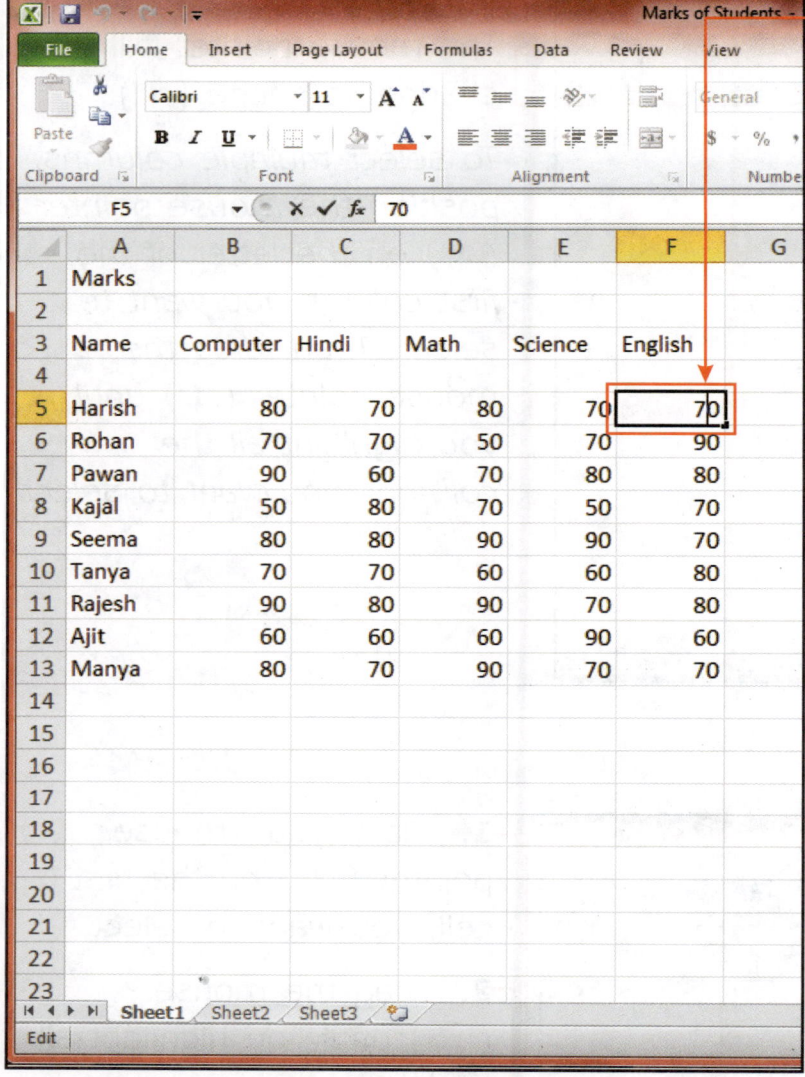

1. Double-click on the cell containing the data you want to edit.

A flashing insertion point appears in the cell.

2. Press the **arrow** keys in the keyboard to move the insertion point to where you want to remove or add characters.

3. To remove a character to the left of the flashing insertion point, press the **Backspace** key.

To remove a character to the right of the flashing insertion point, press the **Delete** key.

4. To add data where the insertion point flashes on your screen, type the data.

5. When you finish making changes to the data, press the **Enter** key.

DELETING DATA IN WORKBOOK

You can remove unrequired data from cells in your worksheet. You can delete data from a single cell or from several cells at once.

1. Select the cell or cells containing data you want to delete.

2. Press the **Delete** key from the keyboard.

The data in the cells you selected disappears.

To deselect cells, click on any cell.

MS-Excel 2010

MOVING AND COPYING DATA

You can move or copy data to a new location in your worksheet.

Moving data allows you to re-organize data in your worksheet. When you move the data, it disappears from its original location.

Copying data allows you to repeat data in your worksheet without having to retype the data. When you copy the data, it appears both in the original and new locations.

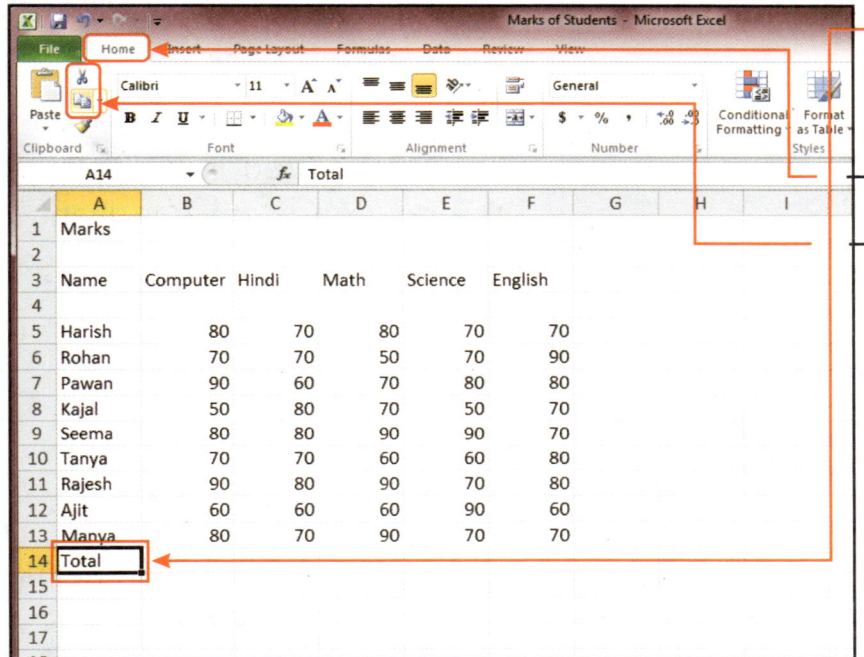

1. Select the cell or cells containing data you want to move or copy.

2. Click on the **Home** tab.

3. Click on one of the following buttons:

   Move text (✂)

   Copy text (📋)

   In this example we choose Copy text, so the text will remain in its original location.

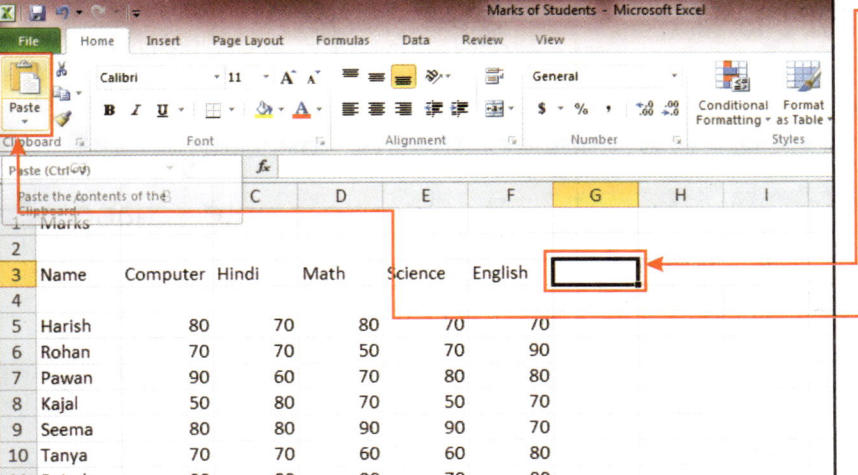

4. Click on the cell where you want to place data.

5. Click on the **Paste** (📋) button to place data in new location.

Data appears in the new location.

17

Drag and Drop Series

CHANGING COLUMN WIDTH

You may want to adjust the width of columns on a worksheet for displaying data properly.

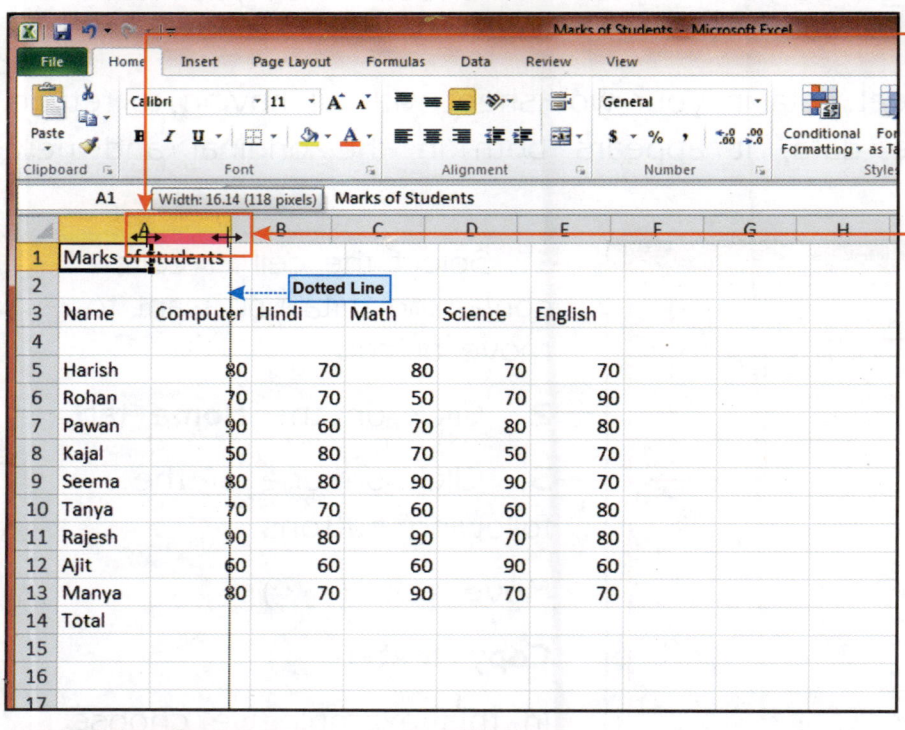

1. To change the width of a column, place the mouse on the right edge of the column heading.

   The mouse pointer changes to (↔).

2. Drag the column edge until the dotted line displays the column width you want.

   The column will display the new width.

CHANGING ROW HEIGHT

You can also change the height of rows besides adjusting the width of columns in your worksheet.

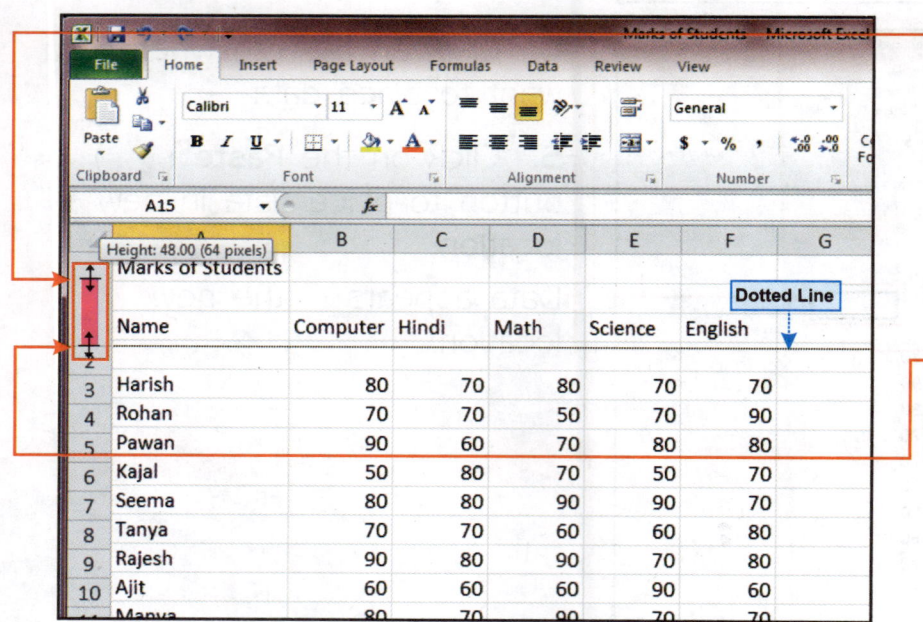

1. To change the height of a row, position the mouse pointer on the bottom edge of the row heading.

   The mouse pointer changes to (⇳).

2. Drag the row edge until the dotted line displays the desired row height.

The row will display the new height.

INSERTING A ROW

You can insert rows in your worksheet. Excel adjusts the cell references to new locations, if the rows that are shifted down include any formula. Thus, if a formula in the cell reference is in row 5 before the insertion, then the cell reference in the formula is adjusted to row 6 after the insertion. **NOTE: Excel will insert a row above the row you select.**

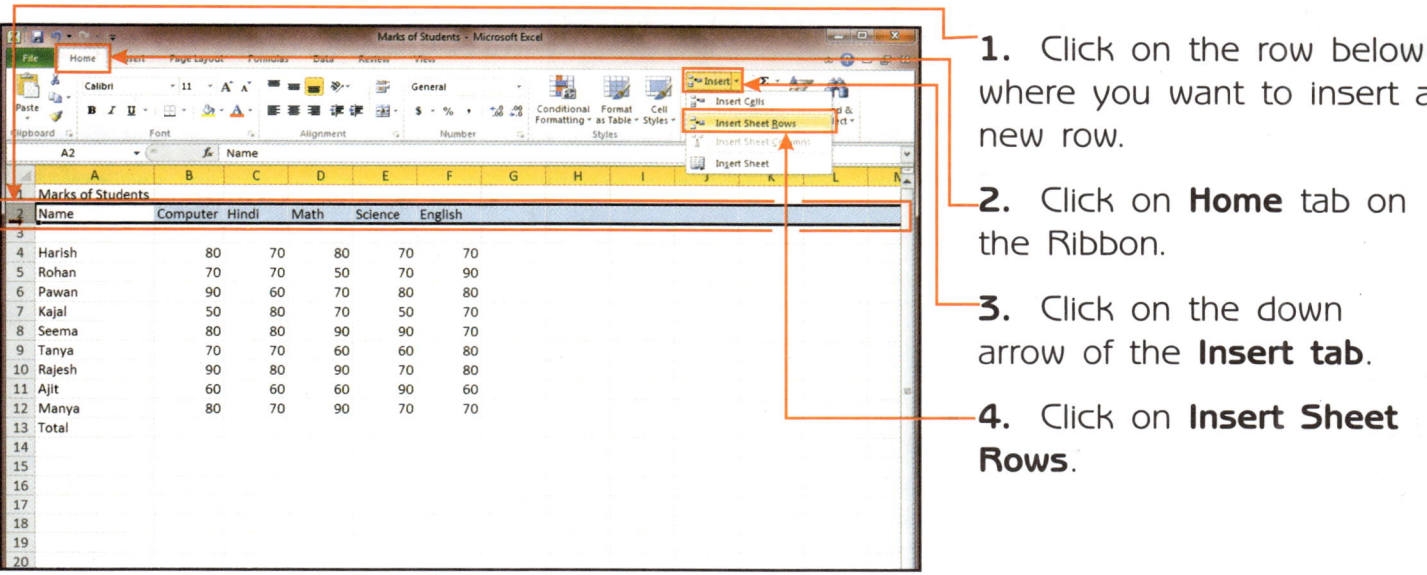

1. Click on the row below where you want to insert a new row.

2. Click on **Home** tab on the Ribbon.

3. Click on the down arrow of the **Insert tab**.

4. Click on **Insert Sheet Rows**.

The new row will appear and all the rows that follow shift downward.

INSERTING A COLUMN

You can add a column to your worksheet to insert additional data. **NOTE: Excel will insert a column to the left of the column you select.**

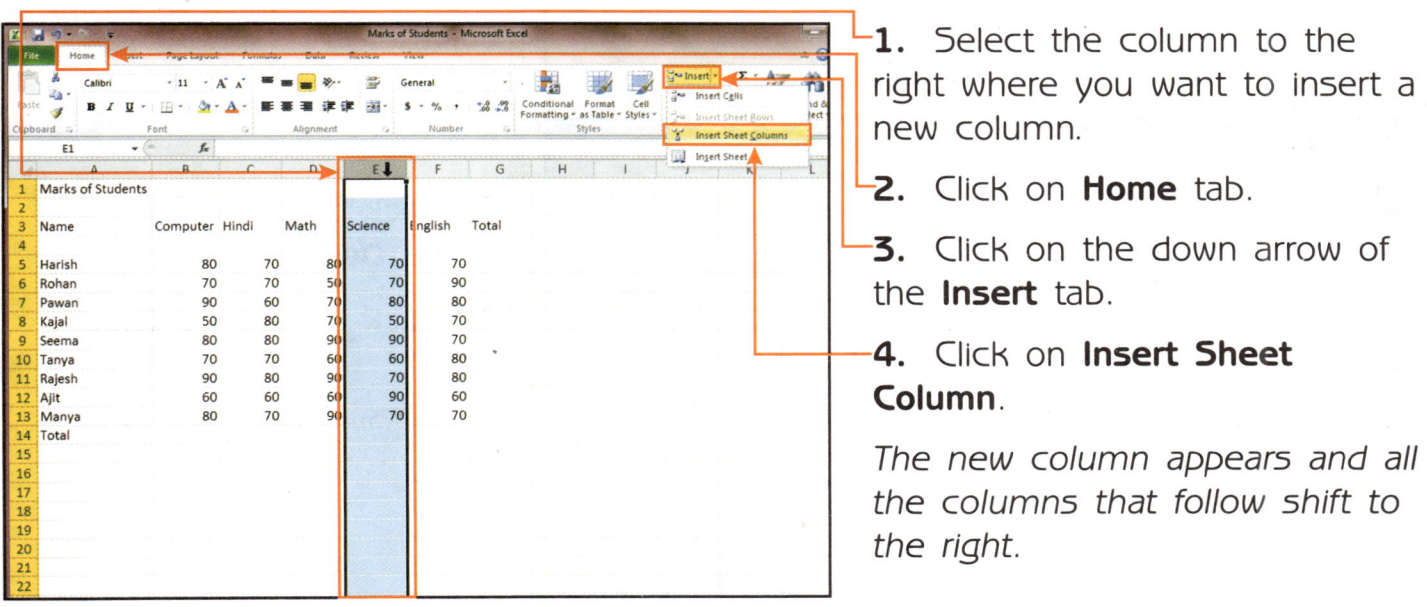

1. Select the column to the right where you want to insert a new column.

2. Click on **Home** tab.

3. Click on the down arrow of the **Insert** tab.

4. Click on **Insert Sheet Column**.

The new column appears and all the columns that follow shift to the right.

Drag and Drop Series

DELETING COLUMN AND ROW

You can remove columns or rows that you no longer need in your worksheet. When you delete an entire column or row, Excel deletes any existing data within the selected cells. Excel also moves over the other columns and rows to fill the space left by deletion.

Delete a column

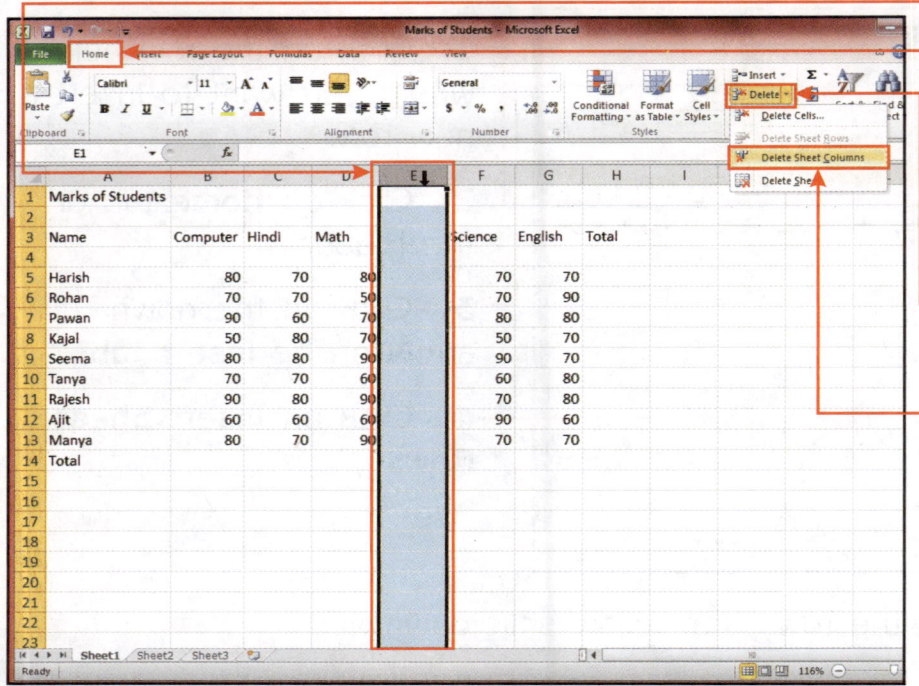

1. Click on the heading of the column that you want to delete.

2. Click on **Home** tab on the Ribbon.

3. Click on the down arrow of the **Delete** tab.

4. Click on **Delete Sheet Column**.

Excel will delete the column.

Delete a row

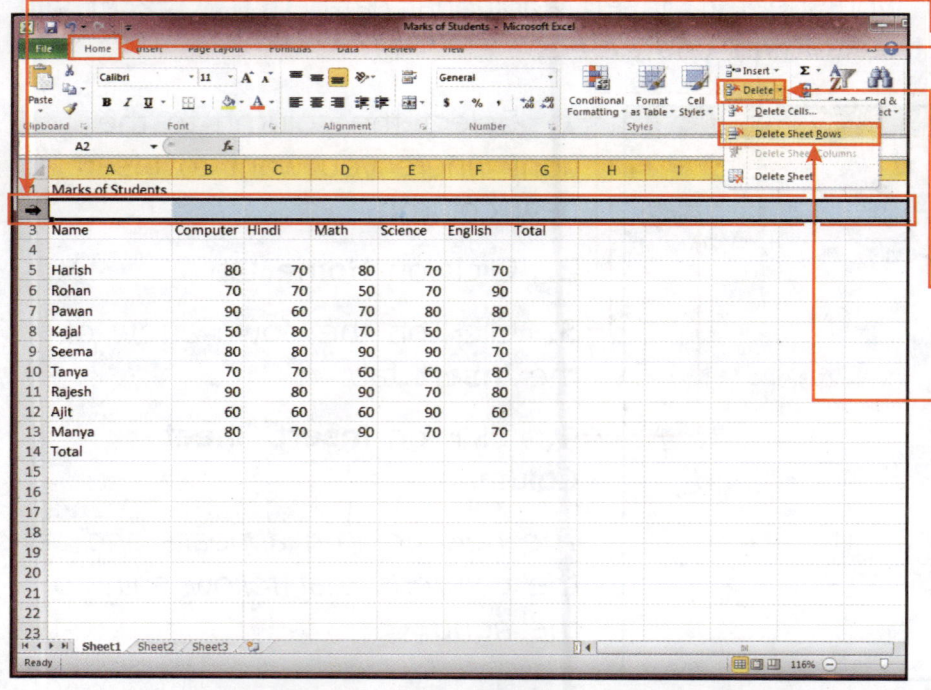

1. Click on the heading of the row that you want to delete.

2. Click on **Home** tab on the Ribbon.

3. Click on the down arrow of the **Delete** tab.

4. Click on **Delete Sheet Row**.

Excel will delete the row.

3 Formatting workbook

FORMATTING WORKBOOK

You can format numbers and text in Excel. Formatting in Excel often goes beyond changing the appearance of the worksheet. These changes may come in the form of a different font set, a font size, bold or italic characters, and many other options. You can give your work a more efficient and professional look by formatting data that is easy to understand.

CHANGING THE FONT OF DATA

You can change the font of data to enhance the appearance of your worksheet.

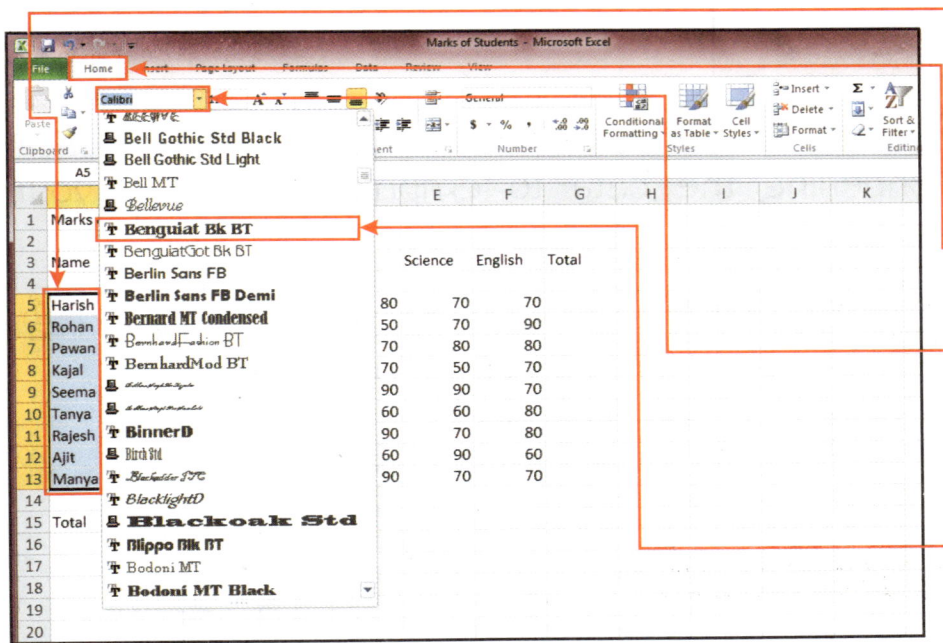

1. Select the cells containing data you want to change to a different font.

2. Click on **Home** tab on the ribbon.

3. Click on the down arrow button of the **Font** tab to display a list of the available fonts.

4. Click on the font you want to use.

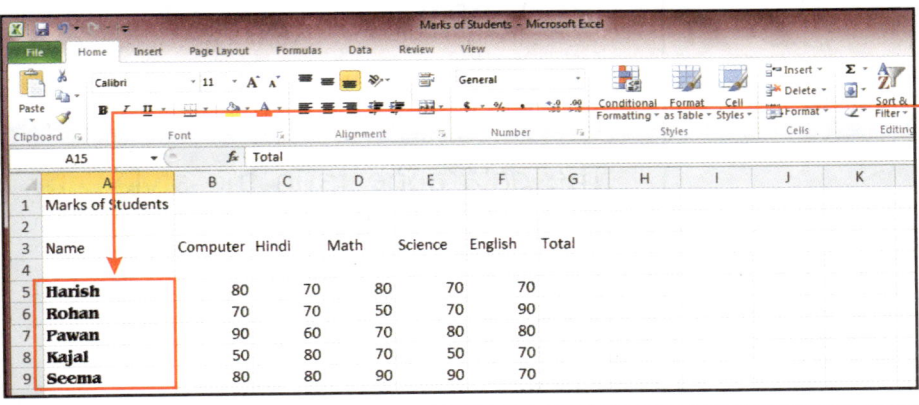

Excel immediately applies the font.

To deselect cells, click on any cell.

Drag and Drop Series

CHANGING THE SIZE OF DATA

You can increase or decrease the size of data in your worksheet.

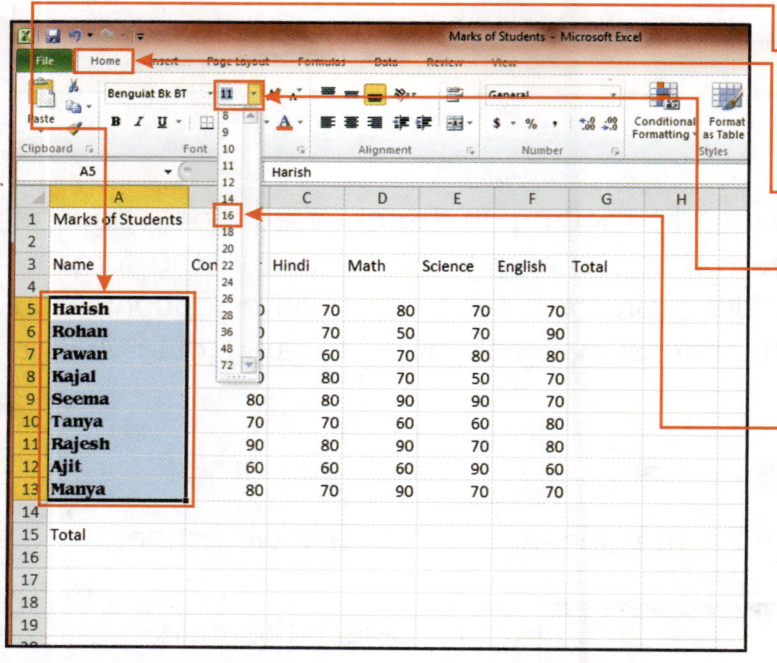

1. Select the cells containing data you want to change to a different font size.

2. Click on **Home** tab on the ribbon.

3. Click on the down arrow button of **Font size** tab to display a list of the available sizes.

4. Click on the size you want to use.

Excel immediately applies the new size.

BOLD, ITALIC AND UNDERLINE DATA

You can bold, italicize or underline the data to emphasize data in your worksheet.

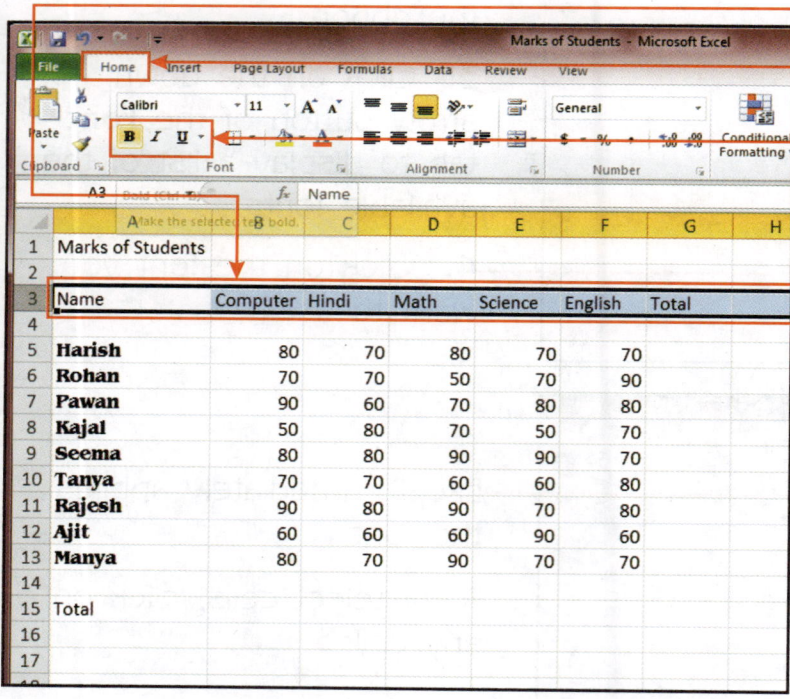

1. Select the cells containing data you want to bold, italicize or underline.

2. Click on **Home** tab on the ribbon.

3. Click on one of the following buttons.

(**B**) **Bold**

(**U**) Italic

(**I**) Underline

The data appears in the style (Bold) you selected.

*To remove a bold, italic or underline style, repeat steps **1** to **3**.*

22

MS-Excel 2010

CHANGING THE ALIGNMENT OF DATA

You can align data in different ways to enhance the appearance of the worksheet.

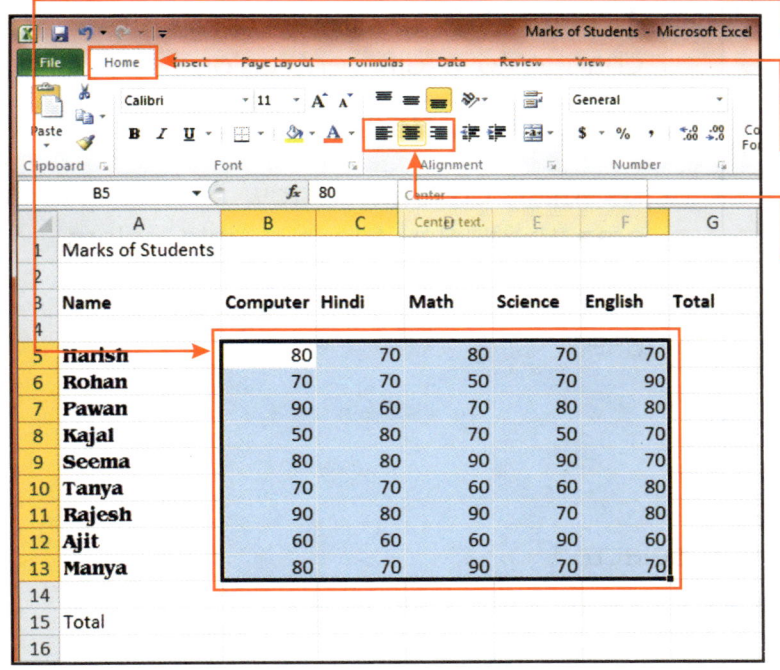

1. Select the cells containing the data you want to align differently.

2. Click on **Home** tab on the ribbon.

3. Click on one of the following buttons.

(▤) Left align

(▤) Center align

(▤) Right align

The data appears in the new alignment.

CHANGING THE COLOR OF DATA

You can change the color of data in your worksheet to draw attention towards headings or important information.

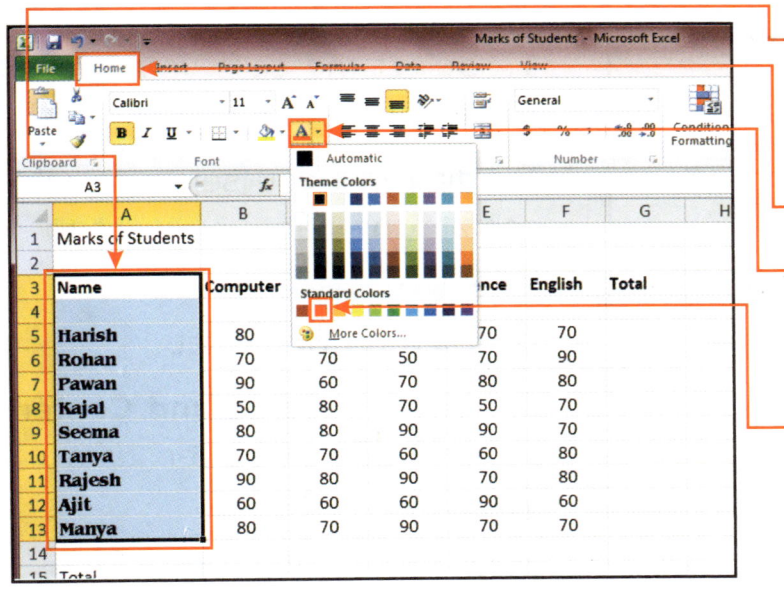

1. Select the cells containing data you want to change to a different color.

2. Click on **Home** tab.

3. Click on down arrow button in this area to display the available colors.

4. Click on the color you want to use.

The data immediately appears in the color you selected.

To return data to its original color, repeat steps **1** to **4**, selecting **Automatic** in step **4**.

23

Drag and Drop Series

CHANGING THE COLOR OF CELL

You can add color to the cells to make them stand out in your worksheet.

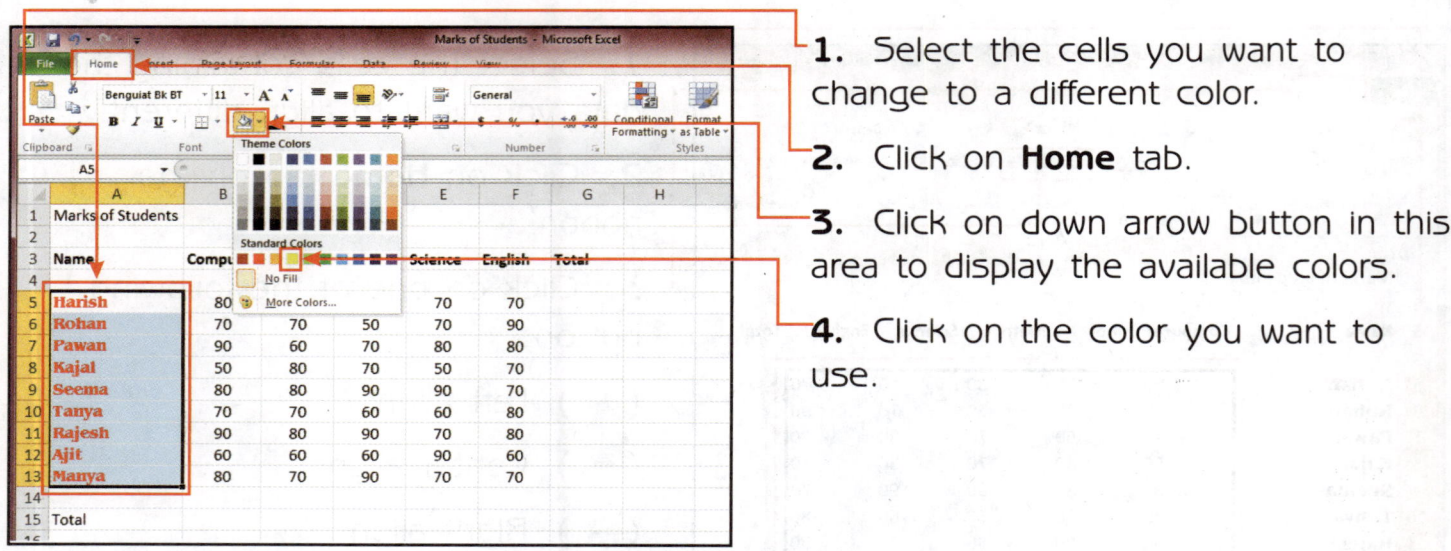

1. Select the cells you want to change to a different color.

2. Click on **Home** tab.

3. Click on down arrow button in this area to display the available colors.

4. Click on the color you want to use.

The cells immediately appear in the color you selected.

To remove color from cells, repeat steps **1** to **4**, selecting **No Fill** in step **4**.

CENTER DATA ACROSS COLUMNS

You can center data across several columns in your worksheet. This is useful for centering titles over your data.

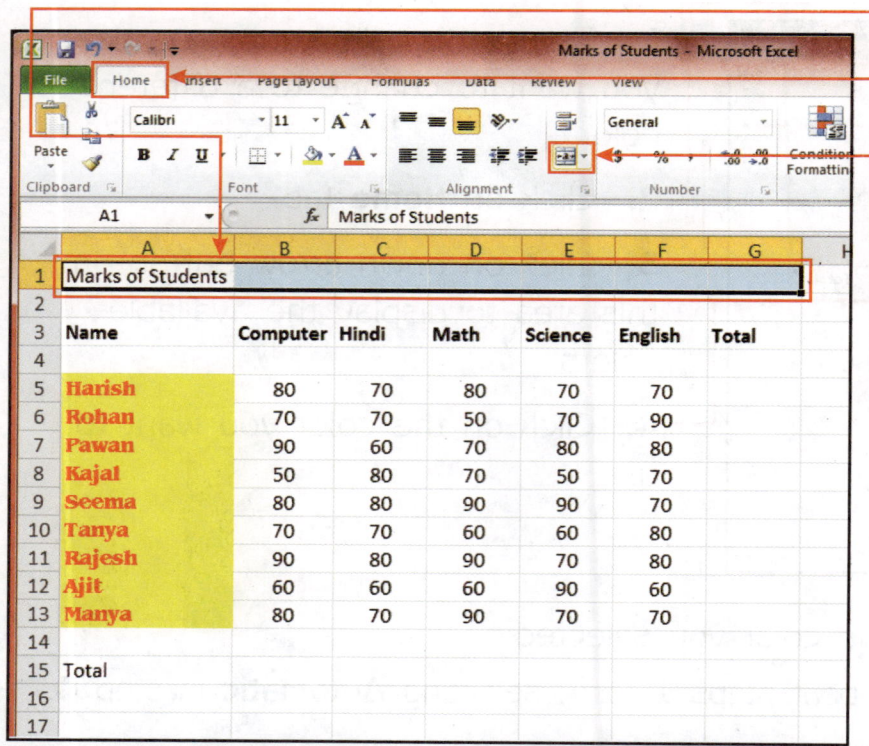

1. Select the cells you want to center the data across.

   The first cell you select should contain the data you want to center.

2. Click on **Home** tab.

3. Click on **Merge and Center** button (▦) to center data across the columns.

   Excel centers data across the columns.

24

ADDING A BORDER

You can add borders to your worksheet cells for defining the contents or to separate the data from surrounding cells more clearly.

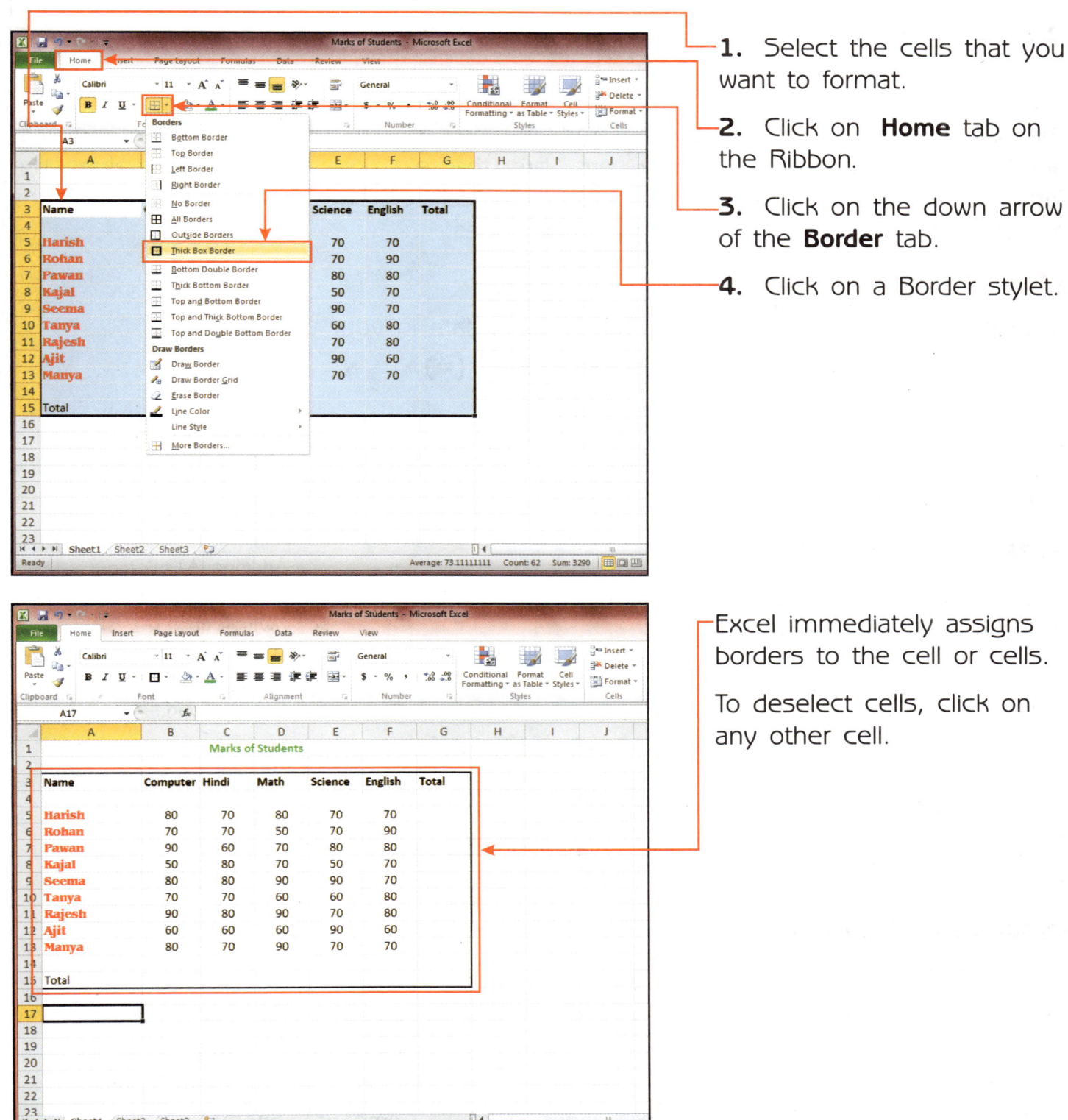

1. Select the cells that you want to format.

2. Click on **Home** tab on the Ribbon.

3. Click on the down arrow of the **Border** tab.

4. Click on a Border stylet.

Excel immediately assigns borders to the cell or cells.

To deselect cells, click on any other cell.

4 Formula and function

In Excel, the data can be of two types : **Constants** and **Formulas**.

The values which are directly entered in the cell are called **constant values**. Numbers, names, data, currency, etc. are the example of constant value. But **formulas** are different. They are a sequence of cell reference, mathematical functions or operators of existing values to give new values.

FORMULA AND FUNCTIONS

A formula allows you to calculate and analyze data in your worksheet.

A formula always begins with an **equal to sign (=)**.

OPERATORS

A formula can contain one or more operators. An operator specifies the type of calculation you want to perform.

Arithmetic operators

You can use arithmetic operators to perform mathematical calculations.

Operator	Description
+	Addition (A1+B1)
-	Subtraction (A1-B1)
*	Multiplication (A1*B1)
/	Division (A1/B1)
%	Percent (A1%)
^	Exponentiation (A1^B1)

Operator	Description
=	Equal to (A1=B1)
>	Greater than (A1>B1)
<	Less than (A1<B1)
>=	Greater than or equal to (A1>=B1)
%	Less than or equal to (A1<=B1)
<>	Not equal to (A1<>B1)

Comparison operators

You can use comparison operators to compare two values. Comparison operators return a value of TRUE or FALSE.

Order of calculations

When a formula contains more than one operator, Excel performs the calculations in a specific order.

You can use parentheses [ ] to change the order in which Excel performs the calculations.

1	Percent (%)
2	Exponentiation (^)
3	Multiplication (*) and Division (/)
4	Addition (+) and Subtraction (-)
5	Comparison operators

Cell references

When entering formulas, use cell references instead of actual data whenever possible. For example, enter the formula =A1 +A2 instead of =10+20.

When you use cell references and you change a number used in a formula, Excel will automatically redo the calculation for you.

FUNCTIONS

A function is a ready-to-use formula that you can use to perform a calculation on the data in your worksheet. Examples of commonly used functions include AVERAGE, COUNT, MAX and SUM.

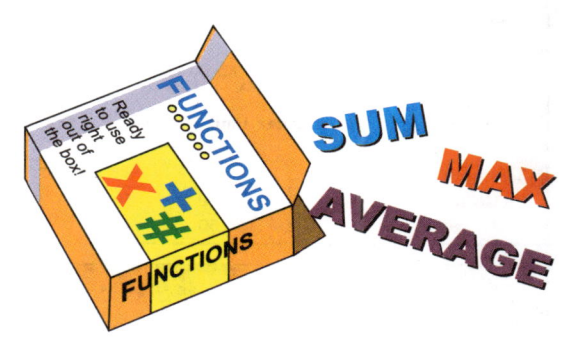

=AVERAGE(A1:A4)
=(10+20+30+40)/4=25

=COUNT(A1:A4) = 4

=MAX(A1:A4) = 40

=SUM(A1:A4)
=10+20+30+40 = 100

- A function always begins with an equal sign (=).
- The data Excel will use to calculate a function is enclosed in parentheses.

Specify individual cells

When a comma (,) separates cell references in a function, Excel uses each cell to perform the calculation. For example, =SUM(A1,A2,A3) is the same as the formula =A1+A2+A3.

Specify a group of cells

When a colon (:) separates cell references in a function, Excel uses the specified cells and all cells between them to perform the calculation.

For example, =SUM(A1:A3) is the same as the formula =A1+A2+A3.

Drag and Drop Series

ENTERING A FORMULA

You can enter a formula into any cell in your worksheet. A formula helps you calculate and analyze data in your worksheet.

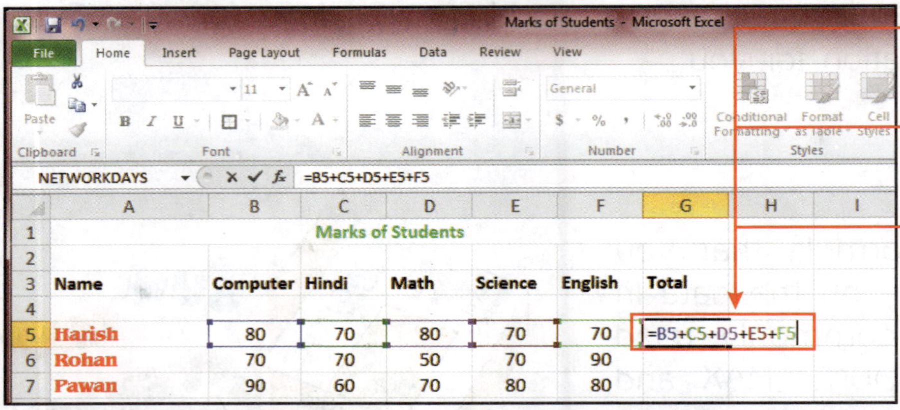

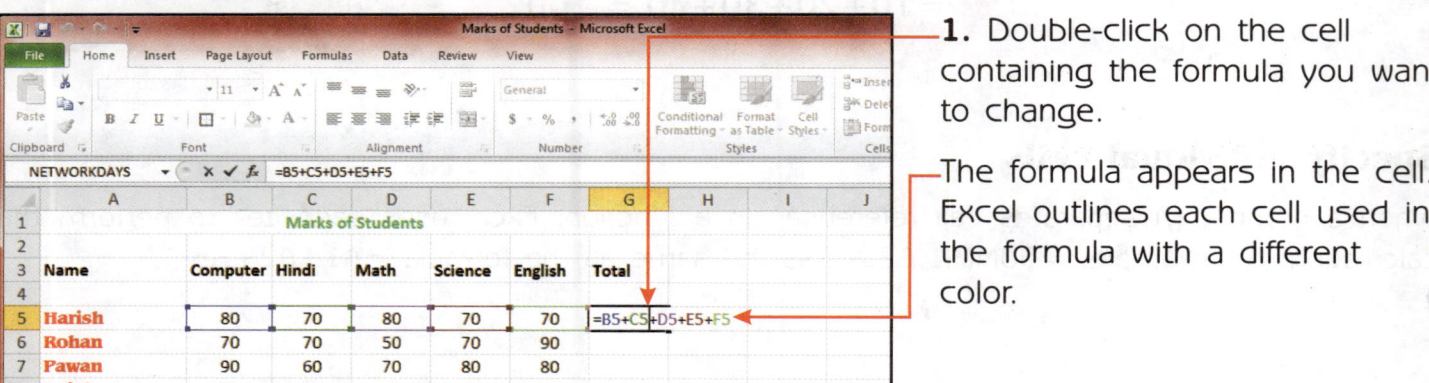

1. Click the cell where you want to enter a formula.
2. Type an equal to (=) sign to begin the formula.
3. Type the formula and then press the **Enter** key.

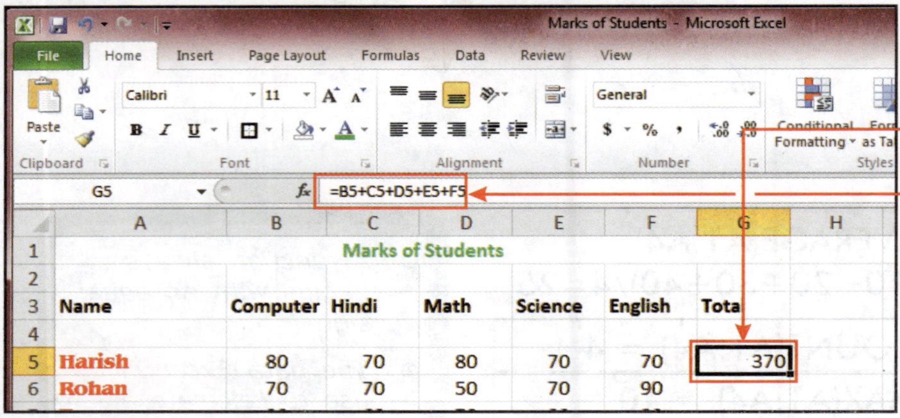

The result of the calculation appears in the cell.

4. To view the formula you have entered, click the cell containing the formula.

The formula bar displays the formula for the cell.

Editing a formula

1. Double-click on the cell containing the formula you want to change.

The formula appears in the cell. Excel outlines each cell used in the formula with a different color.

2. Press the **arrow** key to move the flashing insertion point to where you want to remove or add characters.
3. To add data where the insertion point flashes on your screen, type the data.
4. When you finish making changes to the formula, press the **Enter** key.

28

ENTERING A FUNCTION

Excel helps you enter functions into your worksheet. These functions allow you to perform calculations without typing long, complex formulas.

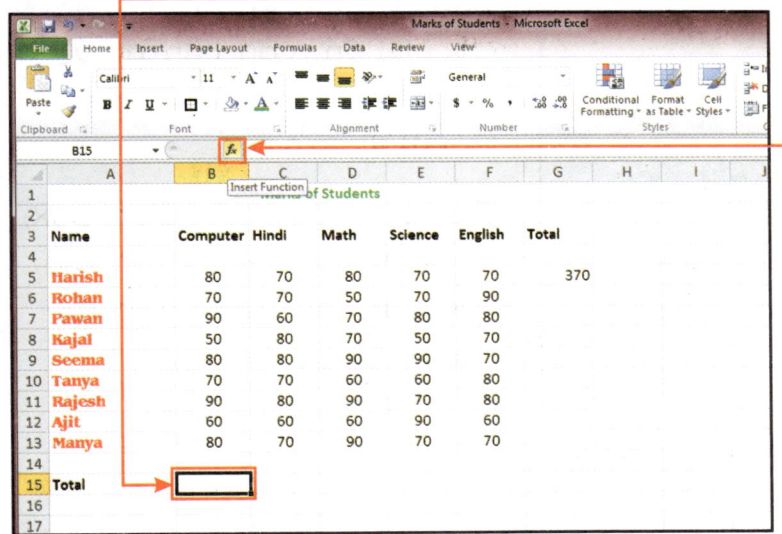

1. Click on the cell where you want to enter a function.

2. Click on **Insert Function** (*fx*) button to enter a function.

   The **Insert Function** dialog box will appear.

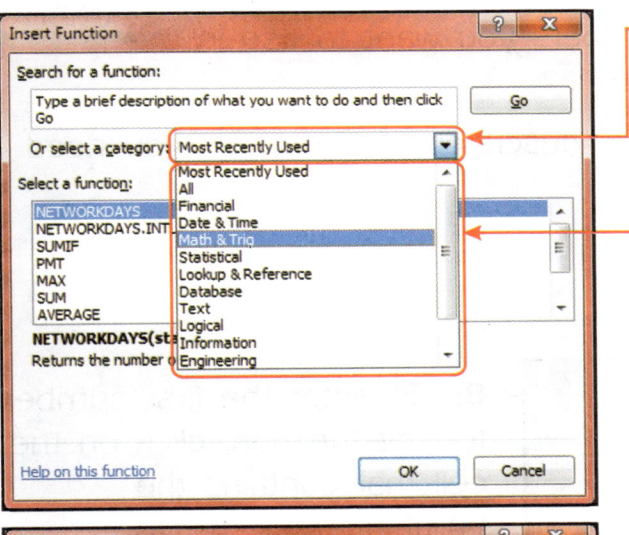

3. Click on the down arrow button to display the categories of available functions.

4. Click on the category containing the function you want to use.

   *If you do not know which category contains the function, select **All** to display a list of all the functions.*

   This area displays the functions in the category you selected.

5. Click the function you want to use.

   This area describes the function you selected.

6. Click **OK** to continue.

Drag and Drop Series

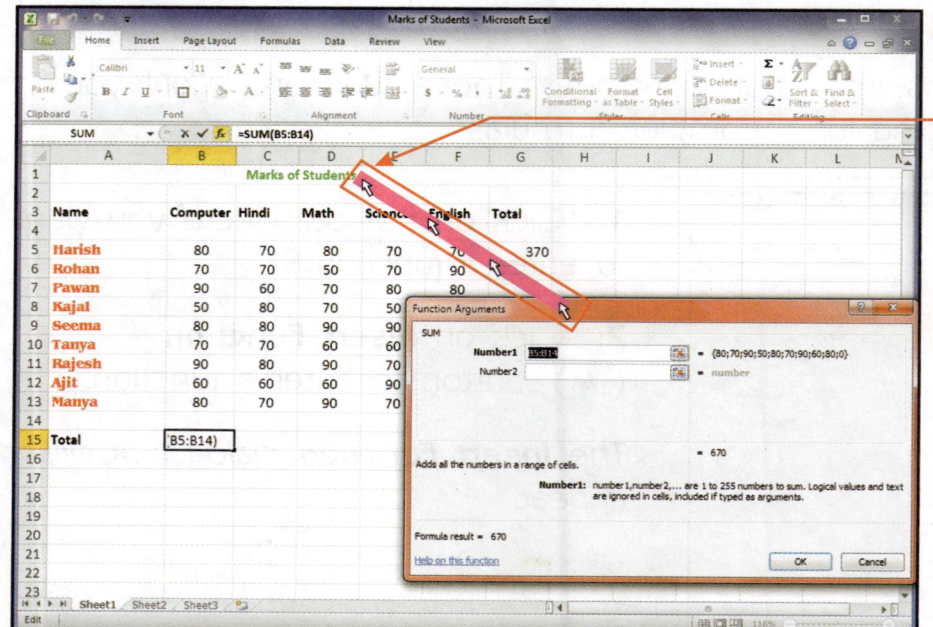

The **Function Arguments** dialog box appears. If the dialog box covers data you want to use in the calculation, you can move the dialog box to a new location.

7. To move the dialog box, position the mouse on the title bar and then drag the dialog box to a new location.

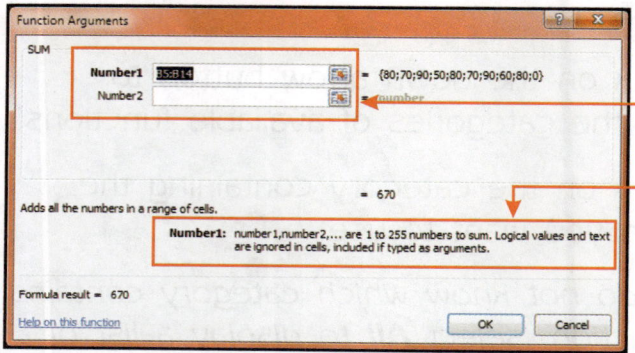

This area displays boxes where you enter the numbers you want to use in the calculation.

This area describes the numbers you need to enter.

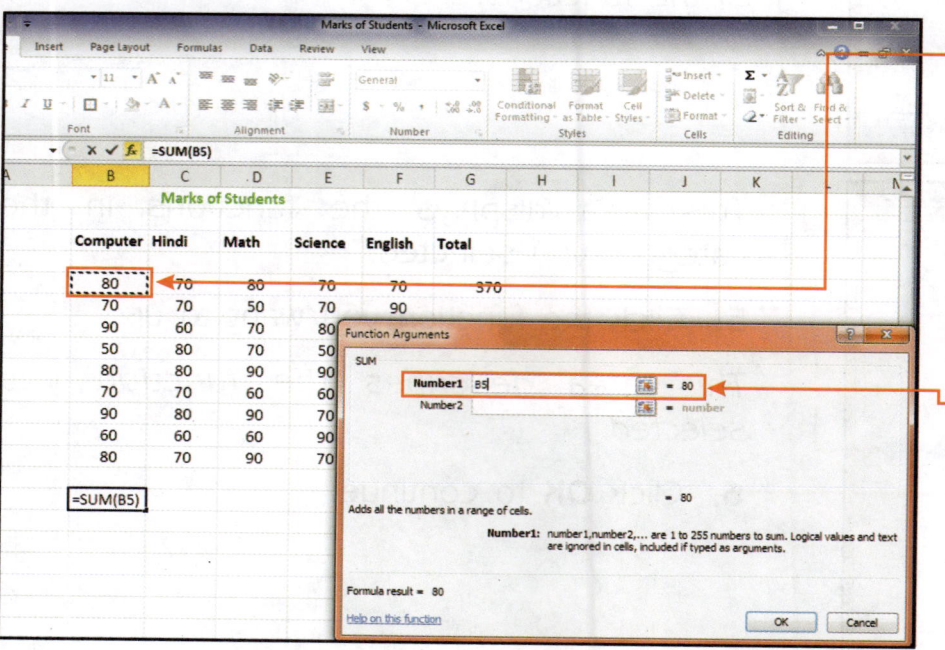

8. To enter the first number for the function, click on the cell that contains the number.

If the number you want to use does not appear in your worksheet, type the number.

The cell reference for the number appears in this area.

30

MS-Excel 2010

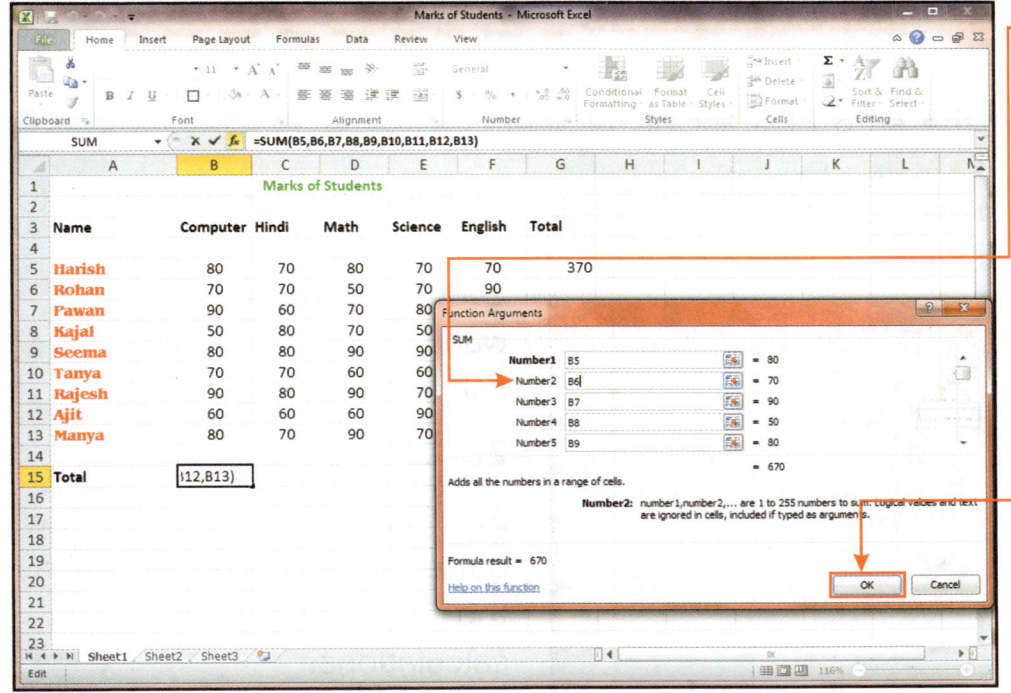

9. Click on the next box to enter the next number.

10. Repeat steps **8** and **9** until you have entered all the numbers you want to use in the calculation.

11. Click on **OK** to enter the function into your worksheet.

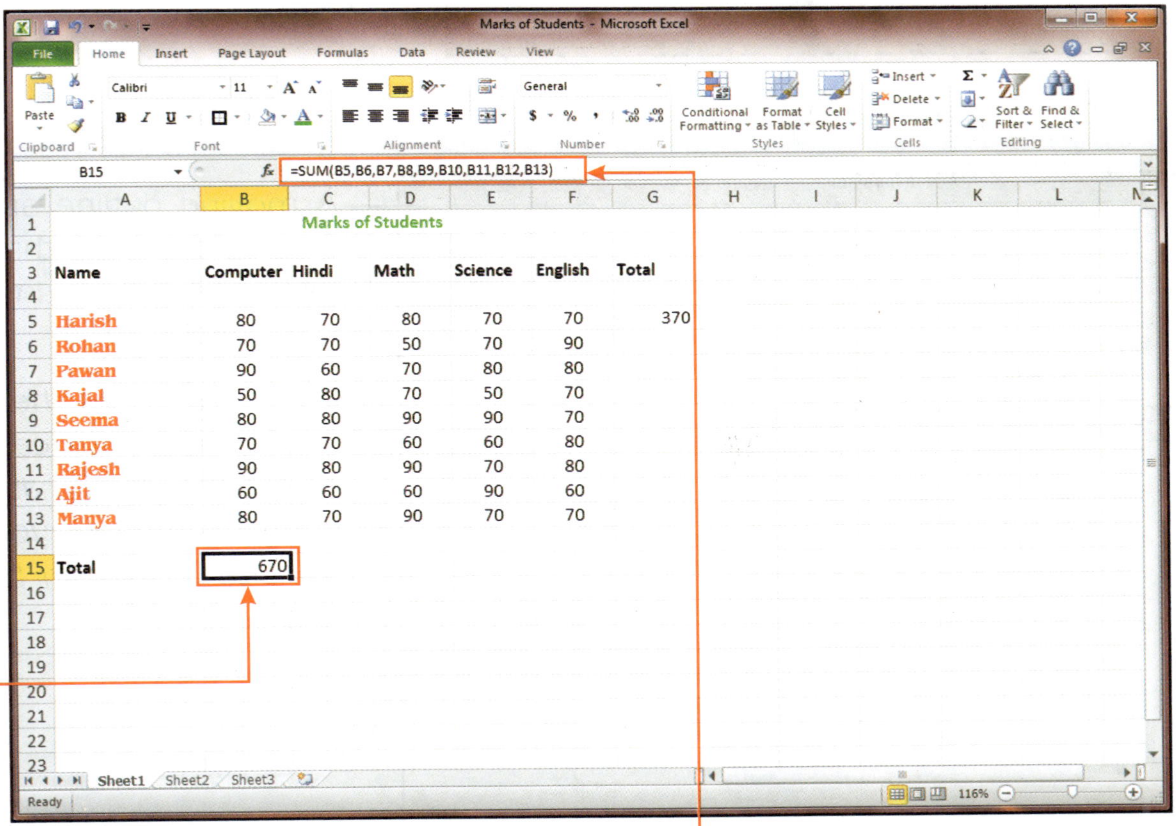

The result of the function appears in the cell.

The Formula bar displays the function for the cell.

Drag and Drop Series

PERFORMING COMMON CALCULATIONS

You can quickly perform common calculations on numbers in your worksheet. For example, you can calculate the sum of a list of numbers.

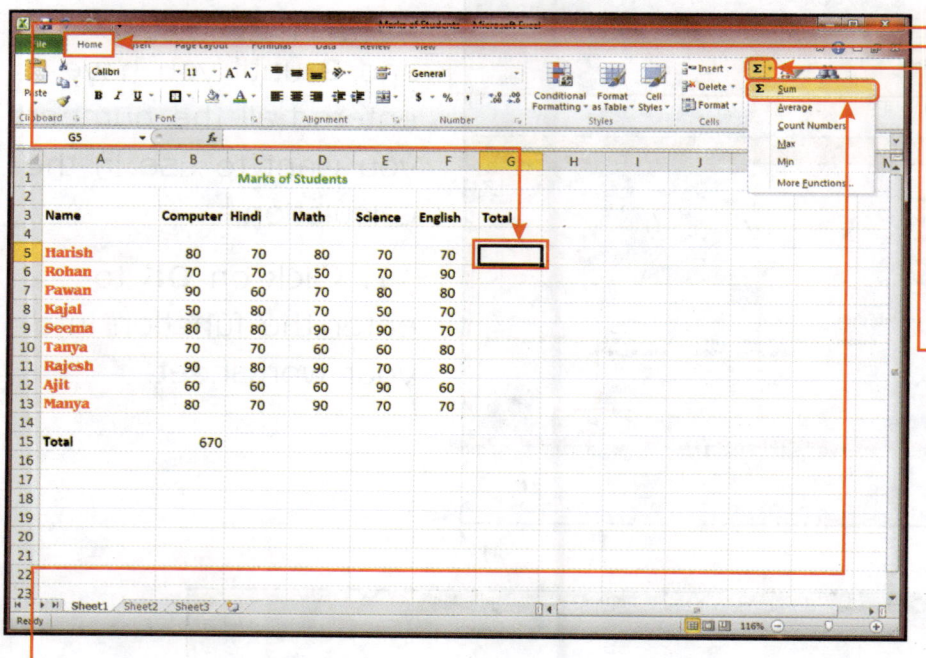

1. Click the cell below or to the right of the cells containing numbers you want to include in the calculation.

2. Click on the **Home** tab.

3. Click on the down arrow button of this area to display the list of common calculations.

4. Click on the calculation you want to perform.

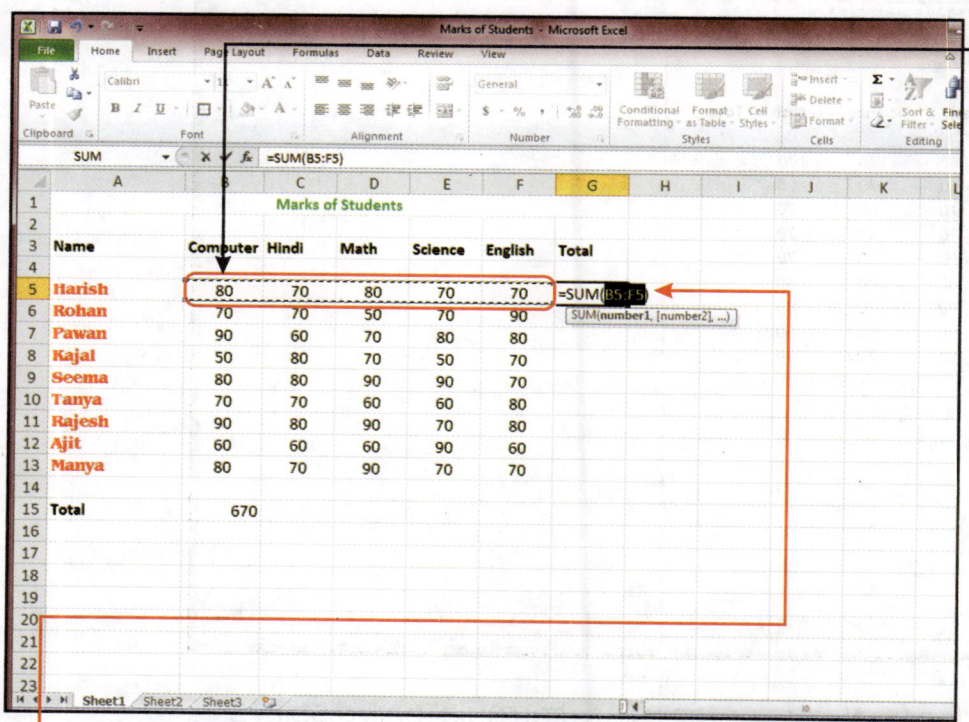

A moving outline appears around the cells that Excel will include in the calculation.

If Excel outlines the wrong cells, you can select the cells that contain numbers you want to include in the calculation.

The cell you selected in step *1* displays the function Excel will use to perform the calculation.

32

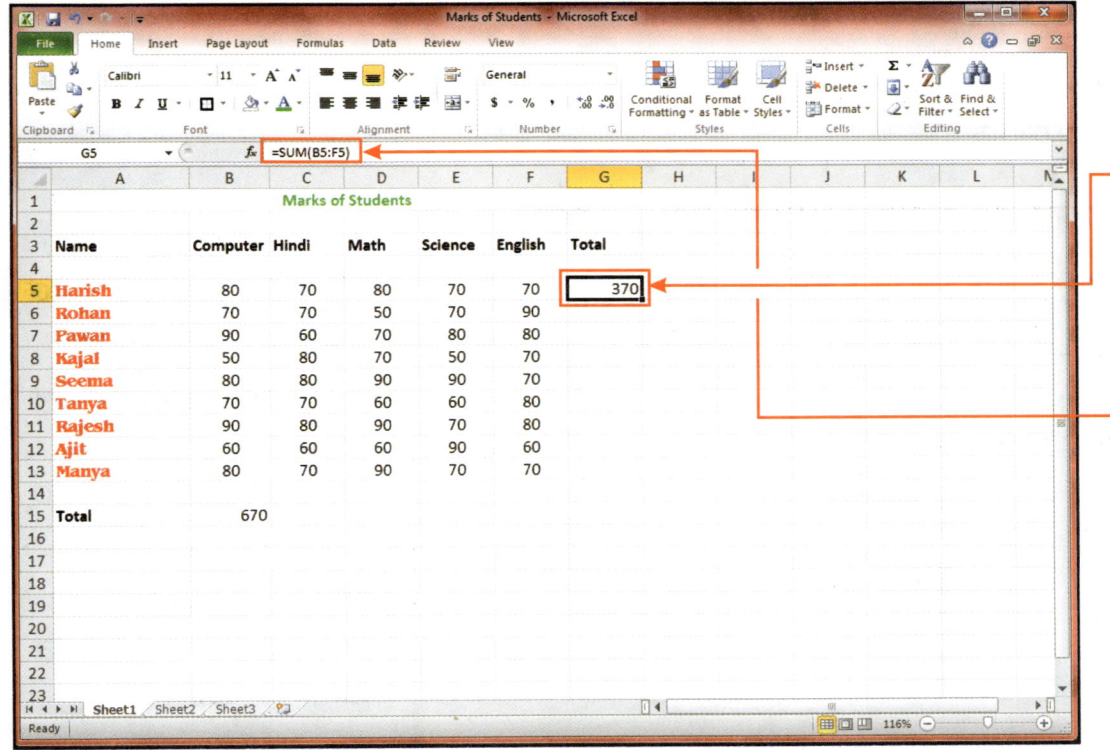

4. Press the **Enter** key to perform the calculation.

The result of the calculation will come in the cell you selected in step **1**.

The Formula bar shows the formula of calculation.

ADDING NUMBERS QUICKLY

You can quickly display the sum of a list of numbers without entering a formula into your worksheet.

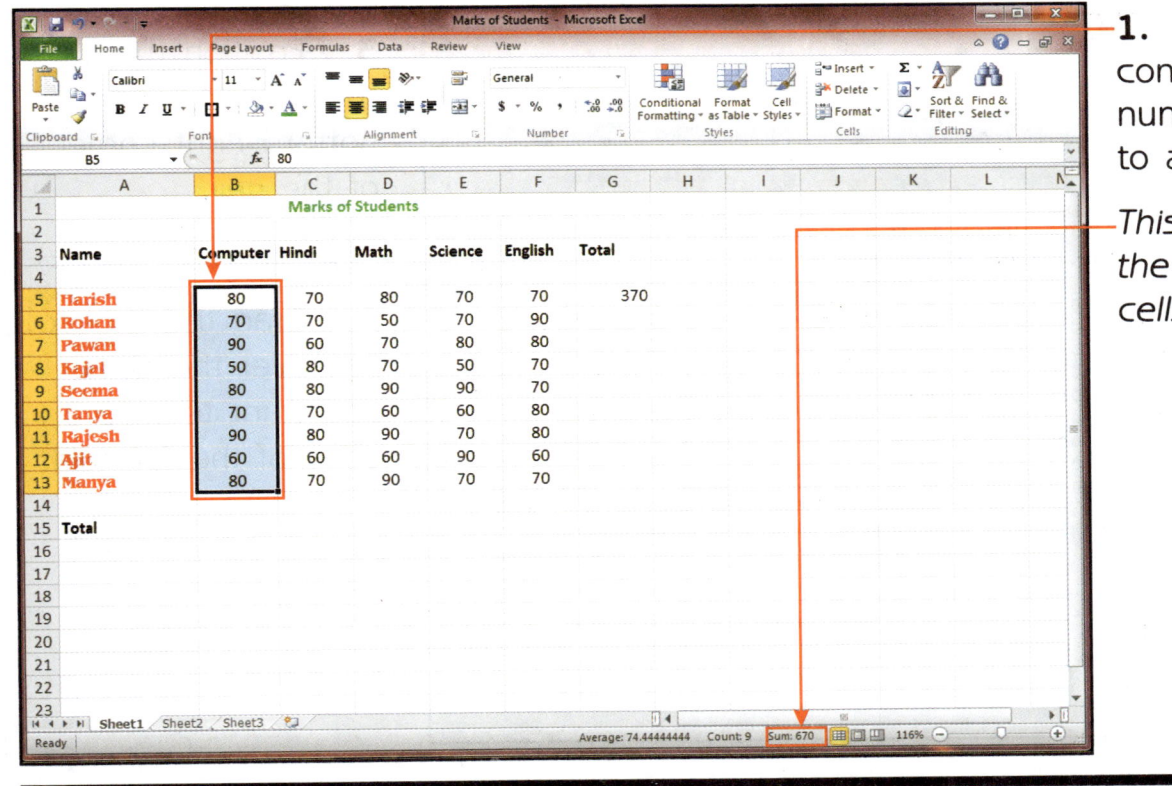

1. Select the cells containing the numbers you want to add.

This area displays the sum of the cells you selected.

Drag and Drop Series

COPYING A FORMULA

If you want to use the same formula in your worksheet several times, you can save time by copying the formula.

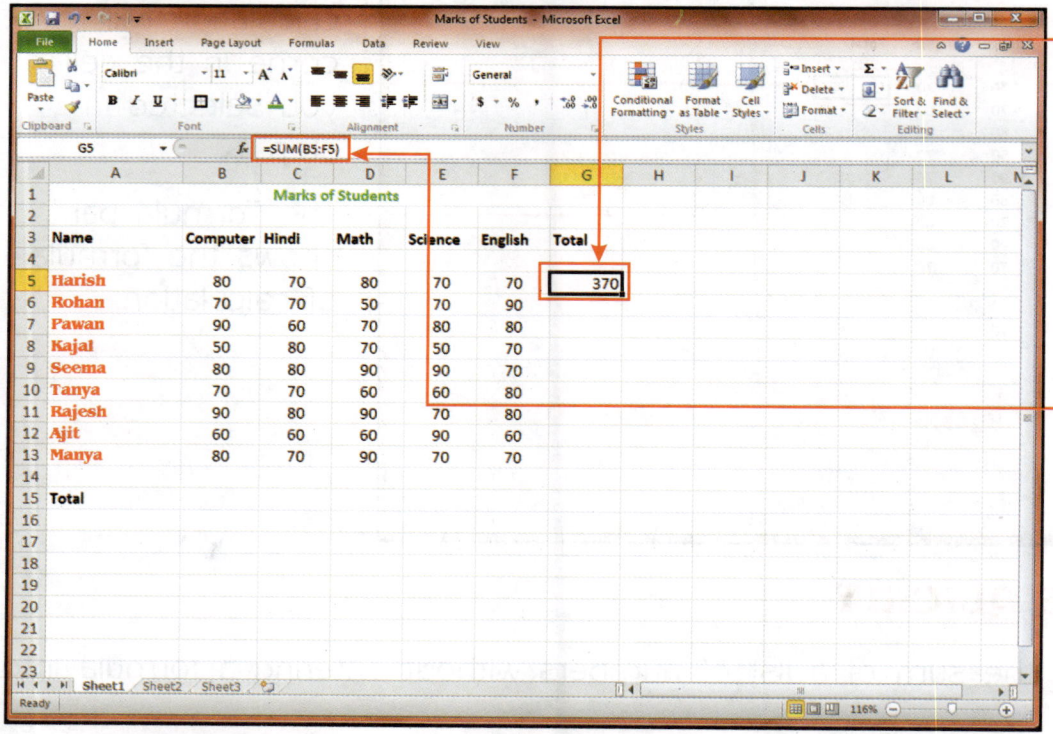

1. Enter the formula you want to copy to other cells.

2. Click on the cell containing the formula you want to copy.

   The formula bar displays the formula for the cell.

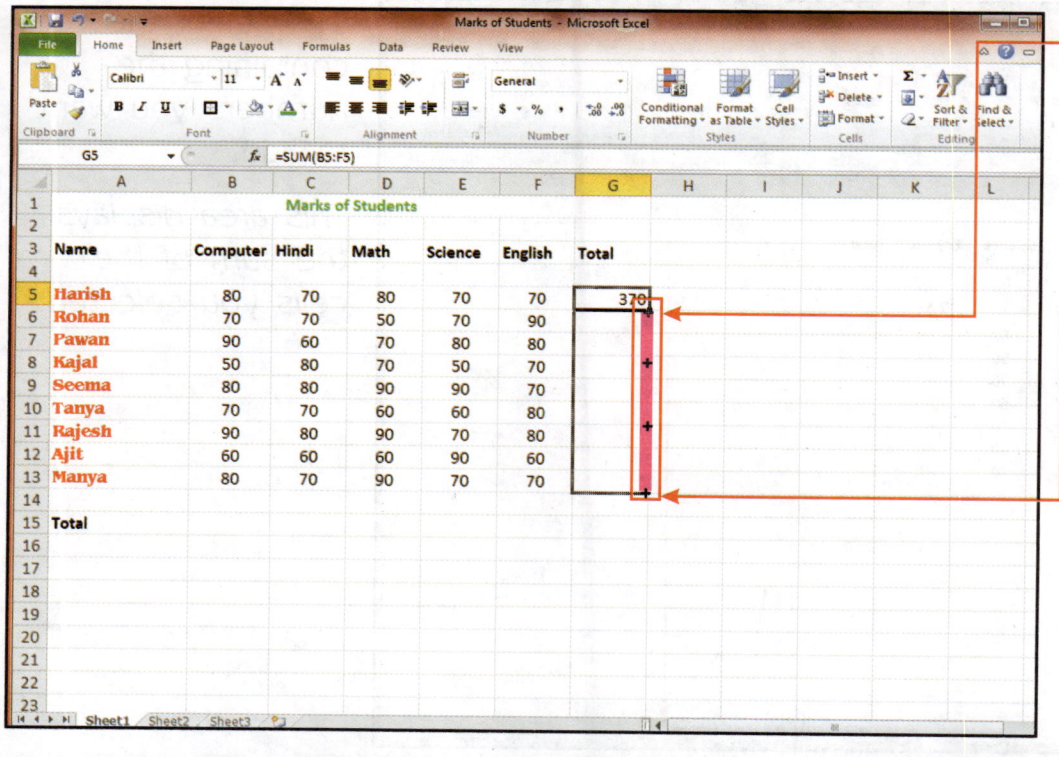

3. Position the mouse (⊕) on the bottom right corner of the cell.

   (⊕) changes to (+).

4. Drag the mouse (+) over the cells you want to give a copy of the formula.

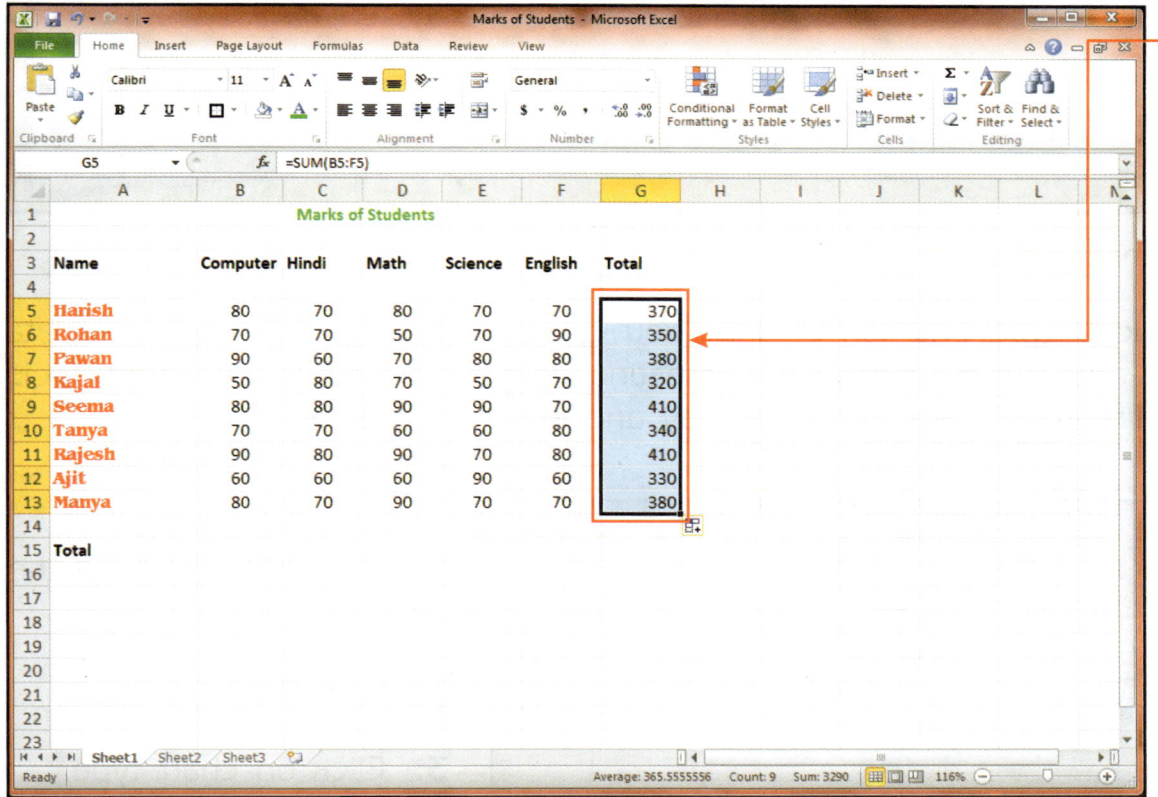

The results of the formulas appear.

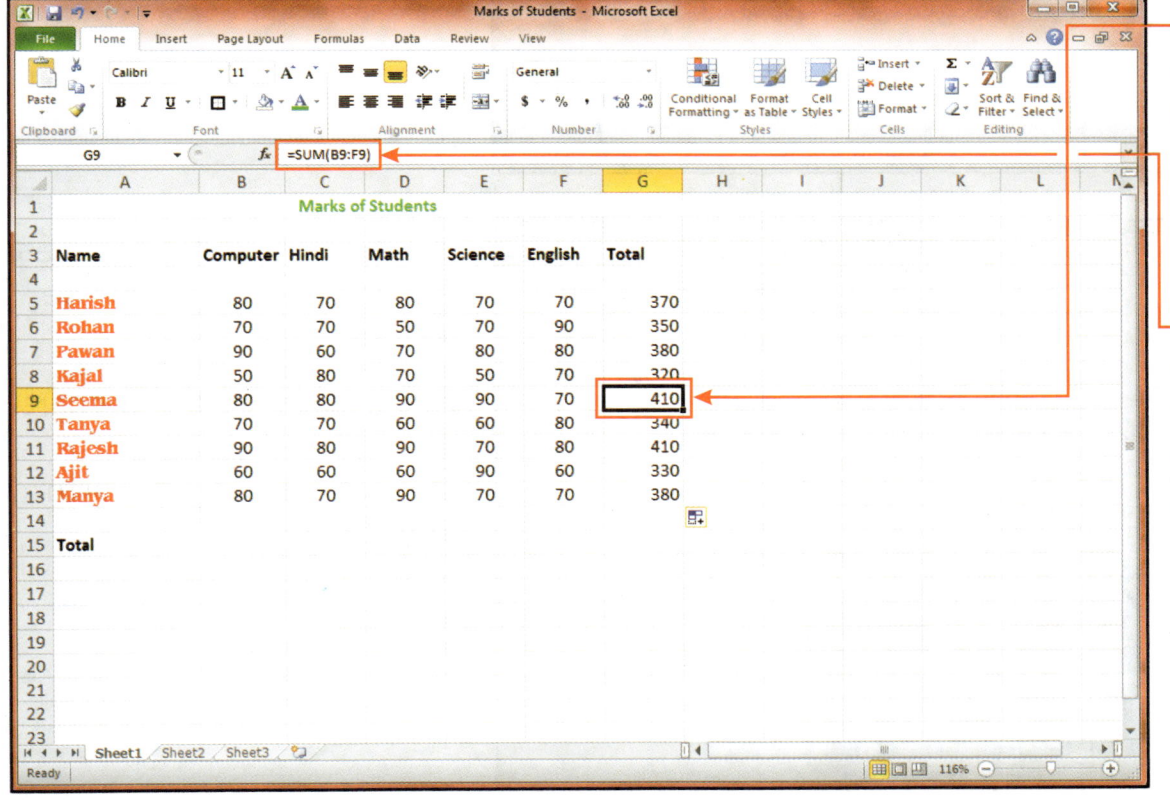

5. To view one of the new formula, click a cell that received a copy of the formula.

The formula bar displays the formula with new cell references.

5 Charts in excel

CREATING A CHART

A chart is a graphical representation of data. You can create a chart to compare data and view patterns and trends easily. After creating a chart, you can use Chart Tools on the Ribbon to fine-tune the chart to display and explain the data.

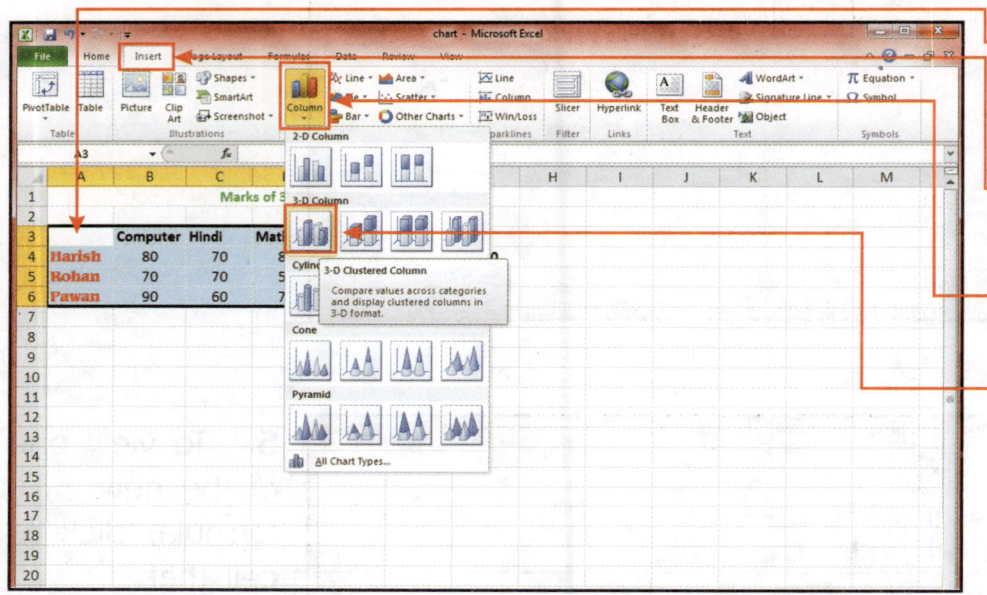

1. Select the range of data that you want on the chart.
2. Click on **Insert** tab on the Ribbon.
3. Click on chart type from the Charts group.
4. Click on chart style.

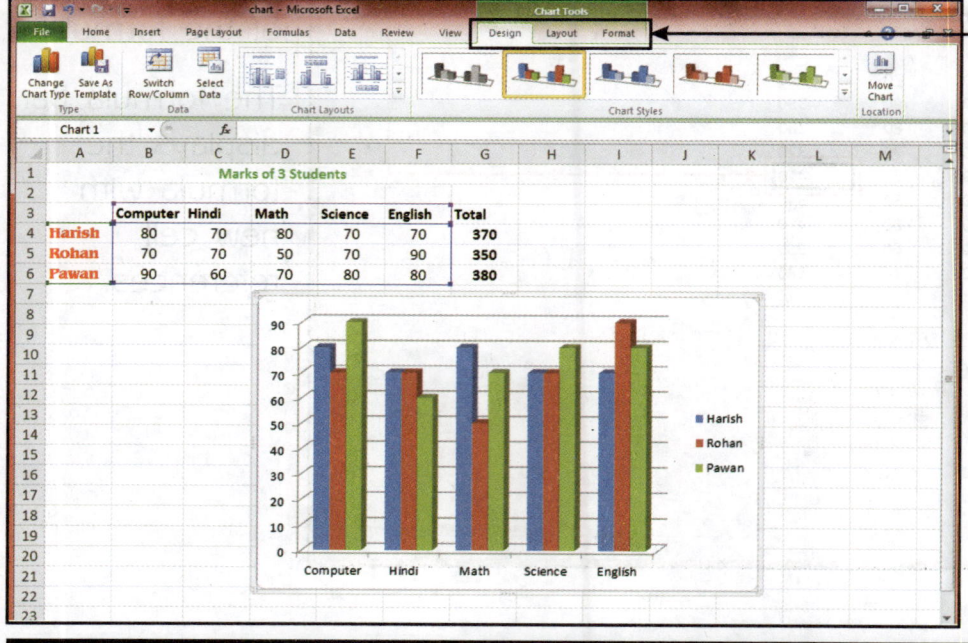

Excel immediately creates a chart, places it on the worksheet.

Excel displays three chart tabs (Design, Layout, Format) for working with the chart.

MS-Excel 2010

CHANGING THE TYPE OF CHART

You can change the chart type to present your data more effectively after creating a chart.

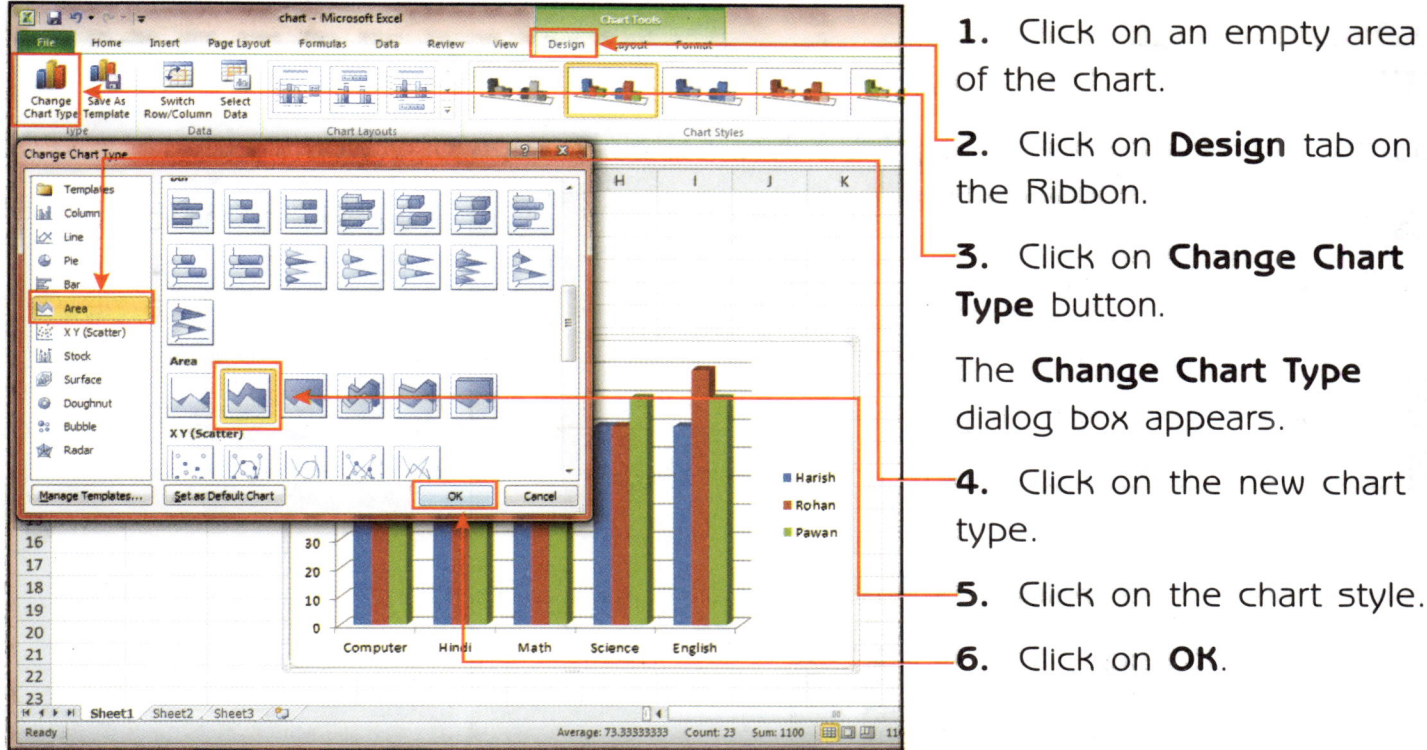

1. Click on an empty area of the chart.
2. Click on **Design** tab on the Ribbon.
3. Click on **Change Chart Type** button.

The **Change Chart Type** dialog box appears.

4. Click on the new chart type.
5. Click on the chart style.
6. Click on **OK**.

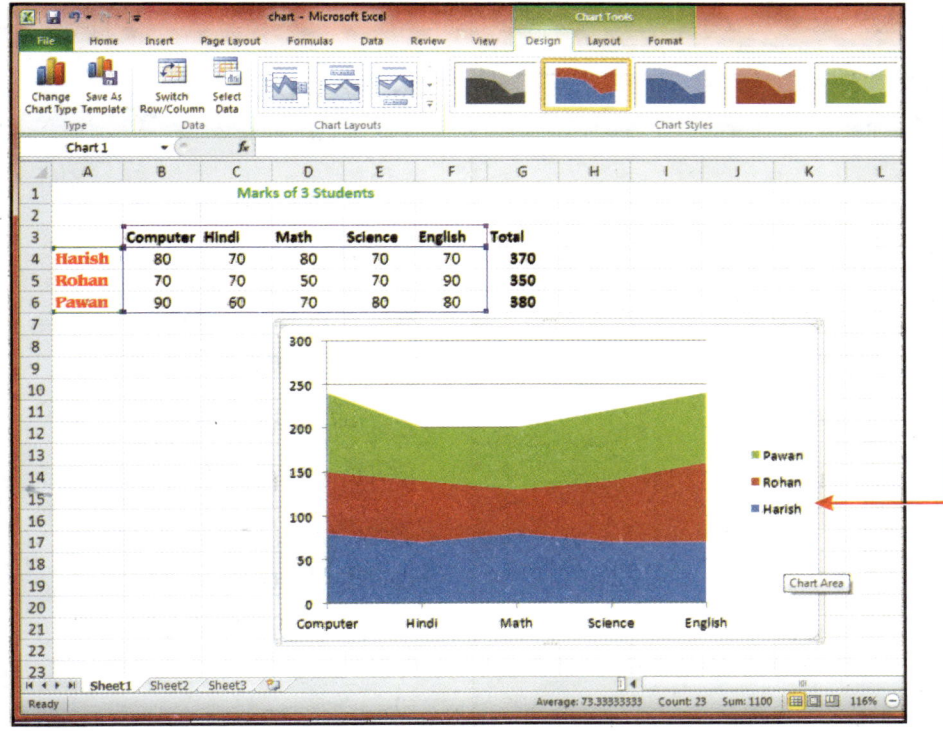

Excel changes the chart to the chart type that you have selected.

6 Printing worksheet

DEFINING PRINT AREA

You can define a print area to print only a certain portion of a worksheet.

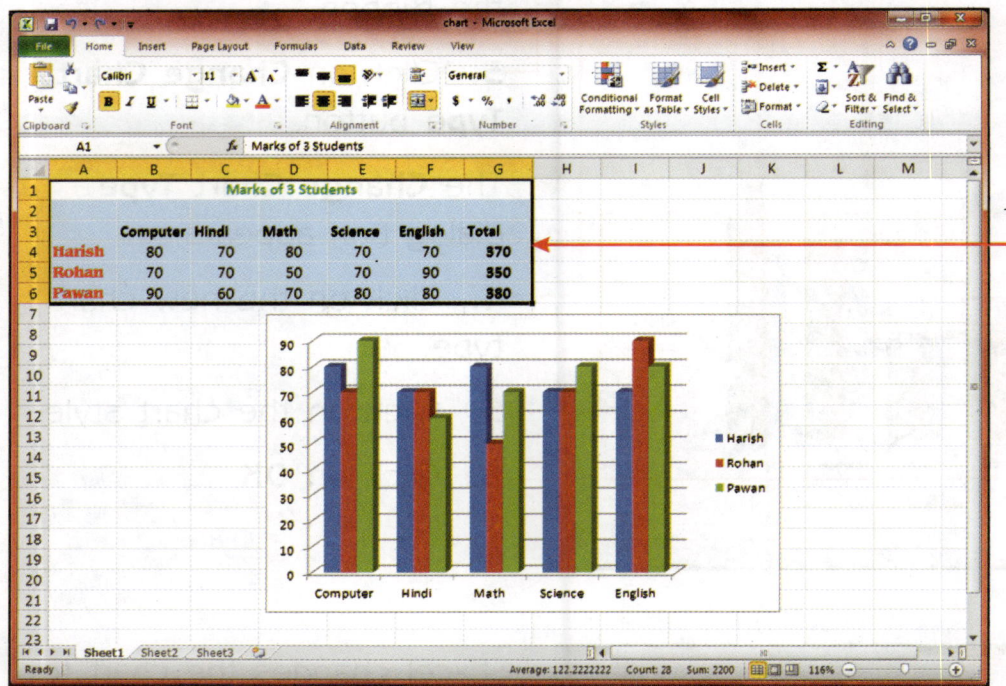

1. Select the cells you want to include in the print area.

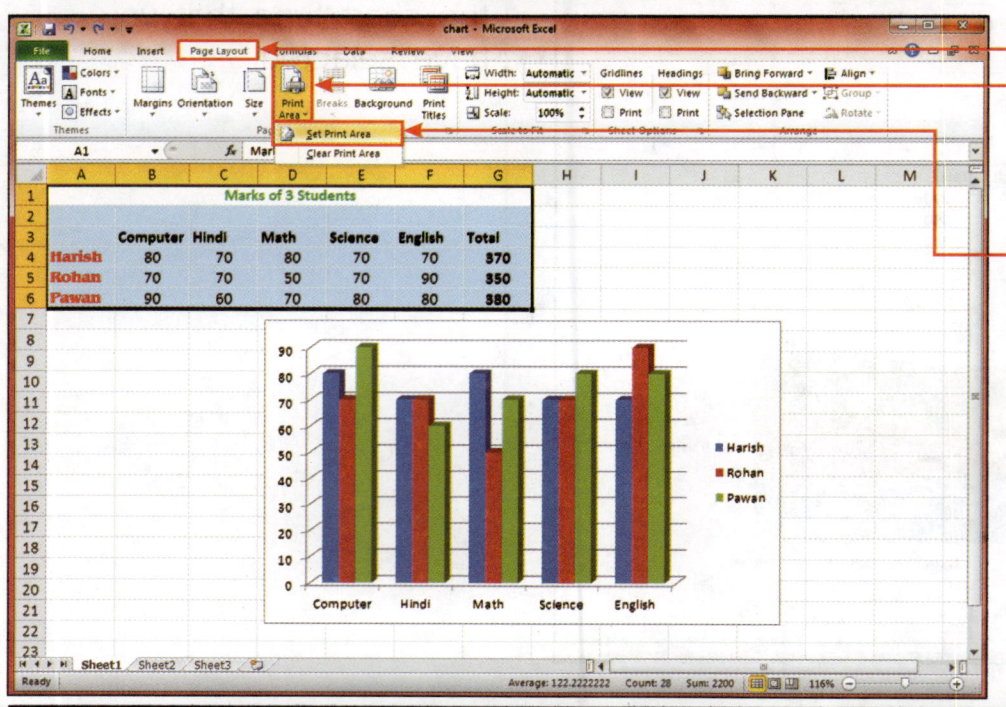

2. Click on **Page Layout** tab.

3. Click on **Print Area**.

4. Click on **Set Print Area**.

Excel saves the print area.

The next time you print, Excel prints only the defined cells.

MS-Excel 2010

PRINTING A WORKBOOK

You can produce a paper copy of the Worksheet displayed on your screen. Before printing your document, make sure that the printer is turned on.

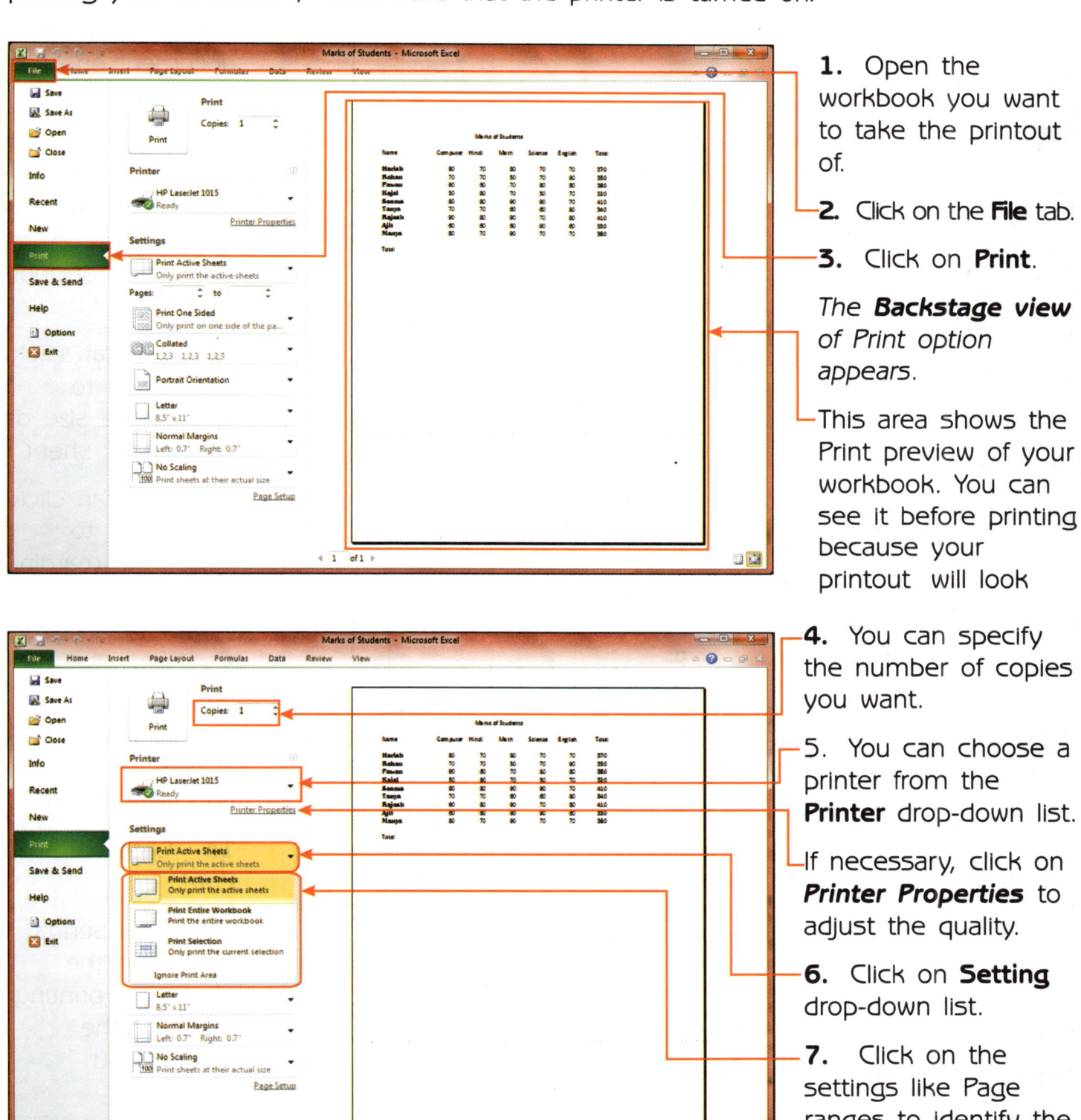

1. Open the workbook you want to take the printout of.

2. Click on the **File** tab.

3. Click on **Print**.

*The **Backstage view** of Print option appears.*

This area shows the Print preview of your workbook. You can see it before printing because your printout will look

4. You can specify the number of copies you want.

5. You can choose a printer from the **Printer** drop-down list.

If necessary, click on **Printer Properties** to adjust the quality.

6. Click on **Setting** drop-down list.

7. Click on the settings like Page ranges to identify the pages you want to print.

Drag and Drop Series

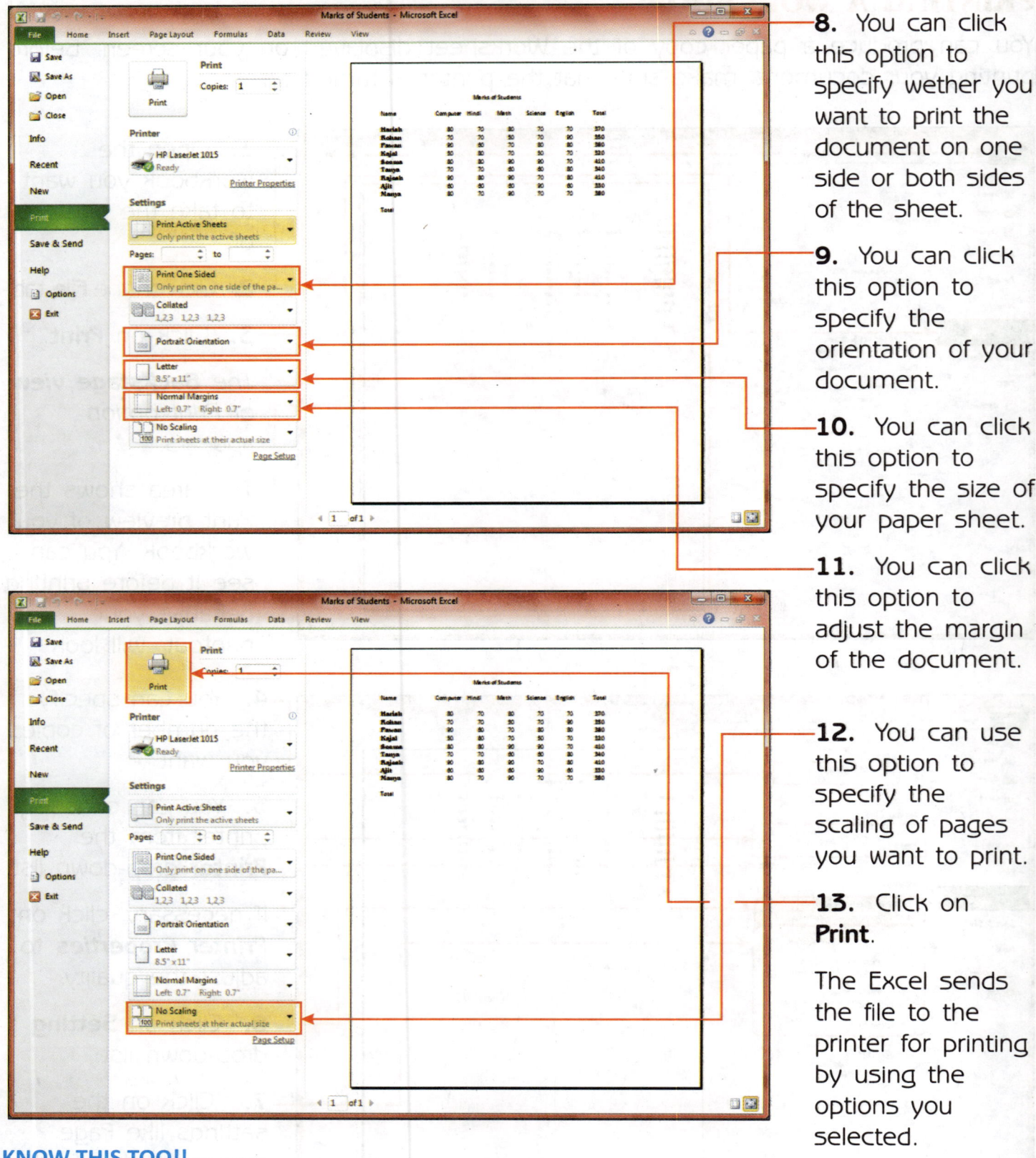

8. You can click this option to specify wether you want to print the document on one side or both sides of the sheet.

9. You can click this option to specify the orientation of your document.

10. You can click this option to specify the size of your paper sheet.

11. You can click this option to adjust the margin of the document.

12. You can use this option to specify the scaling of pages you want to print.

13. Click on **Print**.

The Excel sends the file to the printer for printing by using the options you selected.

KNOW THIS TOO!!

The Print feature in Excel 2010 now enables you to preview, adjust, and print all in the same screen in Backstage view.